SpeakEasy Spanis

Survival Spanish
for
Social Services

Myelita Melton, MA

SpeakEasy Communications, Incorporated

SpeakEasy's Survival Spanish for Social Services

Author: Myelita A. Melton
Cover Design: Ellen Wass Beckerman
Published by SpeakEasy Communications, Incorporated
116 Sea Trail Drive
Mooresville, NC 28117-8493
USA

ISBN 10   0-9786998-8-2
ISBN 13   978-0-9786998-8-8

Survival Spanish for Social Services
Table of Contents

Using This Material

Welcome to *SpeakEasy's Survival Spanish for Social Services*. This material is for adults with no previous experience in the Spanish language. Through research and interviews with professionals in your field, we have developed this material to be a practical guide to using Spanish on the job. Wherever possible, we have chosen to use the similarities between English and Spanish to facilitate your success.

Throughout the manual you will find study tips and pronunciation guides that will help you to say the words correctly. In the guides, we have broken down the Spanish words for you by syllables, choosing English words that closely approximate the Spanish sound needed. This method makes learning Spanish more accessible because it doesn't seem so foreign. When you see letters that are **BOLD** in the guide, say that part of the word the loudest. The bold capital letters are there to show you where the emphasis falls in that word.

At SpeakEasy Communications, we believe that *communication* is more important than *conjugation*, and that what you learn must be practical for what you do. We urge you to set realistic, practical goals. Make practice a regular part of your day and you will be surprised at the progress you make!

SpeakEasy's Secrets to Learning Spanish

Congratulations on your decision to learn Spanish! This decision is one of the smartest choices you will ever make considering the increasing diversity in our country. It's definitely one you will never regret. You are now among a growing number of America's visionary leaders, who want to build more trusting relationships with Hispanic-Americans, the fastest growing segment of our nation's population.

Learning Spanish is going to open many doors for you, and it will affect you in ways you can't imagine. By learning Spanish, you will be able to work more efficiently and safely in almost every workplace in the nation. Since bilingual employees are currently in short supply nationwide, you will find increasing job opportunities in almost every profession. In addition, you will be able to build stronger relationships with Latinos you meet anywhere you go. There's also another added benefit: You are going to raise your communication skills to a whole new level.

As an adult, learning a new language requires a certain mind set. It takes time, patience and more than a little stubbornness. Think about it. You didn't learn English overnight. You began crying as an infant. That was your first attempt at communication. Later you uttered syllables. When you did, your parents thought you were the world's smartest child, and they rewarded you constantly. After a few years you began to make simple sentences. By the time you reached your first class in school, if you were like me, you couldn't stop talking. So, you can't expect to know everything about Spanish by studying it for only a few weeks. You must give Spanish time to sink in just like English did.

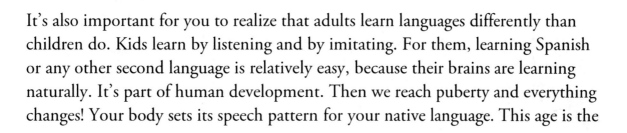

It's also important for you to realize that adults learn languages differently than children do. Kids learn by listening and by imitating. For them, learning Spanish or any other second language is relatively easy, because their brains are learning naturally. It's part of human development. Then we reach puberty and everything changes! Your body sets its speech pattern for your native language. This age is the time when the body's language learning center slows down or turns completely off for many people. Your body just figures it doesn't need it anymore. Coincidentally, this slow-down occurs about the time that you hit your seventh grade Spanish class. That's why learning Spanish seemed to be so hard—that, and the huge amount of very impractical things you were forced to learn. As a result of this physical change in puberty, adults tend to learn languages more visually. Listening and imitating are still important; especially when paired with a visual cue. Most adults benefit from seeing a Spanish word spelled phonetically and hearing it at the same time. This combination helps your brain make sense of the new sounds.

Adults are also practical learners. If you see a reason for what you are learning, you will find it easier to accomplish. It is very true that if you practice your Spanish daily, you are less likely to lose it.

If you did take Spanish in high school or college, you are going to be pleasantly surprised when words and phrases you thought you had forgotten begin to come back to you. That previous experience with other languages is still in your mind. It's just hidden away in a little-used filing cabinet. Soon that cabinet will open up again and that's going to help you learn new words even faster.

Here's another thought you should consider. ***What they told you in the traditional foreign language classroom was not exactly correct.*** There's no such thing as "*perfect Spanish*" just as there is no "*perfect English.*" This fact leaves the door for good communication wide open!

The secret to learning Spanish is having ***self-confidence and a great sense of humor.*** To build self-confidence, you must realize that the entire learning experience is painless and fun. Naturally, you are going to make mistakes. Everyone does. We all make mistakes in English too! So get ready to laugh and learn. ***Don't think that you have to have a perfect Spanish sentence in your head before you say something.*** It's very important for you to say what you know —even if it's only a word or two. The point is to communicate. Communication doesn't have to be "pretty" or perfect to be effective.

Español is one of the world's most precise and expressive languages. Consider these other important facts as you begin to "*habla español*":

- ✓ English and Spanish share a common Latin heritage, so literally thousands of words in our two languages are either *similar* or *identical.*

- ✓ Your ability to communicate is the most important thing, so your grammar and pronunciation don't have to be "*perfect*" for you to be understood.

- ✓ Some very practical and common expressions in Spanish can be communicated with a few simple words.

- ✓ As the number of Latinos in the United States increases, so do your opportunities to practice. Saying even a phrase or two in Spanish every day will help you learn faster.

- ✓ Relax! People who enjoy their learning experiences acquire Spanish at a much faster pace than others.

- ✓ Set realistic goals and establish reasonable practice habits.

- ✓ When you speak even a little Spanish, you are showing a tremendous respect for the Hispanic culture and its people.

- ✓ Even a little Spanish or *poco español* goes a long way!

As you begin the process of learning Spanish, you are going to notice a few important differences. Speaking Spanish is going to feel and sound a little odd to you at first. This feeling is completely normal because you are using muscles in your face that English doesn't require, and your inner ear is not accustomed to hearing you speak Spanish. People tell me it sounds and feels like a cartoon character has gotten inside your head! Don't let that stop you. Just keep right on going!

Many Americans know more Spanish than they realize and they can pronounce many words perfectly. Review the list below. How many of the Spanish words in it, do you recognize? Using what you already know about Spanish will enable you to learn new things easier and faster — it's a great way to build your confidence.

3

Amigos Similares y Familiares

Americano	Amigo	Hospital	Español	Doctor
Loco	Hotel	Oficina	Agua	Fiesta
Dinero	Señor	Señorita	Señora	Sombrero
Burrito	Taco	Olé	No problema	Accidente
Nachos	Salsa	Teléfono	Quesadilla	Margarita
Tequila	Tortilla	Bueno	Grande	Mucho
Blanco	Adiós	Gracias	Feliz Navidad	Hasta la vista
Por favor	Pronto	Sí	Aplicación	Cinco de mayo

The Sounds of Spanish

No se preocupe. Don't worry. One of your biggest concerns about acquiring a new language will be speaking it well enough so that others can understand you. In many ways Spanish is close enough to English that making a few mistakes along the way won't hurt your ability to communicate.

The most important sounds in Spanish consist of *five* vowels. Each one is pronounced the way it is written. Spanish vowels are never *silent*. Even if there are two vowels together in a word, both of them will stand up and be heard.

A	(ah)	as in mama
E	(eh)	as in "hay or the "eh" in set
I	(ee)	as in deep
O	(oh)	as in open
U	(oo)	as in spoon

Here are the other sounds you'll need to remember. Always pronounce them the same way. Spanish is a very consistent language. The sounds the letters make don't shift around as much as they do in English.

4

Spanish Letter		English Sound
C	(before an e or i)	s as in Sam: **cero: SAY**-row
G	(before an e or i)	h as in he: **energía:** n-air-**HE**-ah
		emergencia: a-mare-**HEN**-see-ah
H		silent: **hacienda:** ah-see-**N**-da
J		h as in hot: **Julio, HOO**-lee-oh
LL		y as in yoyo: **tortilla,** tor-**TEE**-ya
Ñ		ny as in canyon: **español,** es-pan-**NYOL**
QU		k as in kit: **tequila,** tay-**KEY**-la
RR		The "trilled" r sound: **burro, BOO**-row
V		v as in Victor: **Victor,** Vic-**TOR**
Z		s as in son: **Gonzales,** gone-**SA**-les

The Other Consonants: The remaining letters in Spanish have very similar sounds to their equivalents in English.

Note: People from Latin American countries have a variety of accents just like Americans do. A variety of accents is common in languages that are spoken over a wide geographic area. In certain areas of Latin America people tend to pronounce the letter "v" more like the English letter "b." This accent is particularly true in some parts of Mexico. In other Latin American countries a "v" sounds like an English "v." If you learned to switch the "v" sound for a "b" sound in high school or college Spanish classes, don't change your habit; however, if you haven't had any experience with Spanish before now, don't sweat the small stuff! Pronounce the "v" as you normally would.

The Spanish Alphabet
El alfabeto español

A	ah	J	HO-ta	R	AIR-ray
B	bay	K	ka	RR	EH-rray
C	say	L	L-ay	S	S-ay
CH	chay	LL	A-yea	T	tay
D	day	M	M-ay	U	oo
E	A or EH	N	N-ay	V	vay
F	f-ay	Ñ	N-yea	W	DOE-blay-vay
G	hay	O	oh	X	A-kees
H	AH-chay	P	pay	Y	ee-gree-A-gah
I	ee	Q	coo	Z	SAY-ta

Did you notice something different about the Spanish alphabet? It has four letters the English alphabet doesn't have. Can you find them?

The Four "Extra" Letters

Look carefully at the table above which contains the Spanish alphabet. Did you notice that the Spanish language has more letters in its alphabet than English does? There are thirty letters in the Spanish alphabet. Even though Spanish has more letters in its alphabet, none of them will present *problemas* for you. Here are the four extra letters and words in which they are used:

CH Sounds like the following English words: Chuck, Charlie, and Chocolate. Try saying these Spanish words: nacho and macho.

6

LL   Sounds essentially like an English "y." However, you will hear slight variations depending on where the person is from who is speaking Spanish to you. **Example**: Tortilla (tor-**T**-ya)

Ñ   Sounds like a combination of "ny" as in canyon or onion. **Example**: español (es-pan-**NYOL**).

RR   This letter is a "trilled" sound. Practice by taking your tongue and placing it in the roof of your mouth just behind your front teeth. Now blow air across the tip of your tongue and make it flutter. This sound can be difficult for some adults to make. It's only strange because you are moving your tongue muscle in a new way. Since there are no words in English with trilled sounds, you just never learned to move your tongue that way. Children learning Spanish have no trouble with this sound at all. Like any new activity, it will take time, patience and practice! Don't let a problem with the trilled "r" stop you from speaking. Essentially the sounds of the English "r" and the Spanish "r" are the same. To start with, say the double "r" a bit louder than a single "r." **Example**: Burrito (boo-**REE**-toe)

The Spanish Accent

In Spanish you will see two types of accent marks. Both marks are very important and do different things. One of the marks you will notice is called a "tilde." It is only found over the letter "N." But, don't get the Ñ confused with N. The accent mark over Ñ makes it into a different letter entirely. In fact, it's one of four letters in the Spanish alphabet that the English alphabet doesn't have. The Ñ changes the sound of the letter to a combination of "ny." You'll hear the sound that this important letter makes in the English words "canyon" and "onion."

Occasionally you will see another accent mark over a letter in a Spanish word. The accent mark or "slash" mark shows you where to place vocal emphasis. So, when you see an accent mark over a letter in a Spanish word, just say that part of the word louder. For example: José (ho-**SAY**). These accented syllables are indicated in your pronunciation guides with bold, capital letters.

Pronouncing Spanish Words

The pronunciation of Spanish words follows very basic, consistent rules. This regular pattern makes it easier to learn. Here are some tips to remember:

1. Most Spanish words that end with vowels are stressed or emphasized on the *next to the last* syllable.

    Señorita: sen-your-**REE**-ta   Jalapeño: ha-la-**PAIN**-yo

2. Look for an accent mark. If the Spanish word has an accent in it, that's the emphasized syllable.

    José: ho-**SAY**   ¿Cómo está?: **CO**-mo es-**TA**

3. Words that end in consonants are stressed on the *final* syllable.

    Doctor: doc-**TOR**   Hotel: oh-**TELL**

Spanish Punctuation Marks

Spanish has two different punctuation marks than English does. Both of them are upside down versions of English punctuation marks. They are used to signal that something besides a simple declarative sentence is ahead.

First, there's the upside down question mark (¿). You will see it at the beginning of all questions. It's there to let you know that what follows is a question and you will need to give your voice an upward inflection. It's the same sort of inflection we use in English.

Example: Do you speak English?   ¿Habla inglés?

Next, there's the upside down exclamation mark (¡). It's there to let you know that what follows should be vocally emphasized.

Example: Hi!   ¡Hola!

Spanglish

Much of the southwestern part of the United States originally belonged to Mexico. In 1848, after the US-Mexican War, the border was moved south to the Rio Grande River. The treaty that was signed at the end of the conflict transformed Spanish-speaking Mexicans into Americans overnight! Imagine waking up one morning and finding out that you are a citizen of another country — and that you have to learn a new language! As a result, an entirely new slang language was born that mixes the best of both worlds: *Spanglish*.

In America, Spanglish really started to come into its own in the early 1970s. At that time it gained both in popularity and vocabulary. Now, people who use Spanglish span generations, classes, and nationalities. It's heard in pop music, seen in print, and used in conversations throughout Latin America. It isn't just an American phenomenon. Immigrants may turn to Spanglish out of necessity while they are learning English, and bilingual speakers use it because it's convenient. If you listen to native speakers carefully, you will hear them use a mixture of languages. Sometimes in the middle of a conversation, you may hear an English word or two. People who speak Spanish tend to use whatever word or phrase suits their purpose and is most descriptive. In general conversation it doesn't matter what language it is. Even though Spanglish is still frowned upon in most traditional language classes and by those who want to keep the Spanish language "pure," it really is a great tool for most people.

Common Spanglish Words

Truck/Trocka	Lunch/Lonche	No parking/No parque
Yard/Yarda	Break/Breaka	Cell phone/Cel
Carpet/Carpeta	Check/Chequear	Market/Marketa
Push/Puchar	Roof/Ruffo	Email/Email

More Amigos Familiares

Using what you've learned about Spanish sounds, practice the words listed below. Examine them carefully. Each word bears a strong resemblance to its English counterpart or it is a common Spanish word. Begin by slowly pronouncing each word on the list. If you are having trouble, go back and review the vowel sounds. Continue by reviewing the section on Spanish accents and pronunciation. Reviewing these concepts will help you as you continue building your skills.

Accidente	Flan	Padre
Aeropuerto	Flor	Paga
Apartamento	Florería	Patata
Aplicación	Fruta	Persona
Avenida	General	Piña
Banana	Gimnasio	Plato
Banco	Hacienda	Policía
Bueno	Hamburguesa	Posible
Café	Hasta mañana	Progreso
Carro	Identificación	Rápido
Caución	Importante	Restaurante
Centro	Interesante	Río
Chocolate	Jalapeño	Rosbif
Conversación	Jamón	Servicio
Dentista	Leche	Súpermercado
Diciembre	Macarrones	Supervisor
Dirección	Mecánico	Té
Discusión	Mesa	Teatro
Espárrago	Minuto	Televisión
Especial	Momento	Tomate
Familia	Motor	Tortilla

Muchos Ways to "Practicar"

The more you listen to and use your *español,* the easier it will be to learn it. There are lots of ways to practice, that won't cost you any money. Try these super techniques for improving your skills:

- ✓ Next time you're at a Mexican restaurant, order your food in *español.*

- ✓ Start slowly. Practice one sound each week.

- ✓ Read Spanish language newspapers. They are usually free and easily available.

- ✓ Listen to Spanish language radio stations.

- ✓ Watch Spanish language television.

- ✓ Rent Spanish language videos; especially cartoons.

- ✓ Buy Spanish tapes and listen to them in the car while you commute.

- ✓ And — speaking of tapes, there is such a variety of Latin *música* available, something will be right for you. Listening to music is a great way to train your ears to Spanish and have fun doing it. Personally, I like anything by Carlos Santana or the Salsa of Marc Anthony. What do you like?

- ✓ Visit Internet sites like *www.about.com* or *www.studyspanish.com.* You can find all kinds of information there about the Spanish language. They have a wonderful, free newsletter that comes to you via e-mail. Most search engines have some sort of Spanish section. An on-line search will turn up lots of treasures!

- ✓ Next time you listen to a baseball game, keep track of all the Hispanic names you hear.

- ✓ Speak Spanish every time the opportunity presents itself. Practice is the only way to get over your nervousness.

- ✓ Try to learn with a friend at work and practice together.

What practice habits work for you? Share them with us at:
info@speakeasyspanish.com

SpeakEasy's Tips and Techniques
for Comunicación

It's important to remember, when you're trying to communicate with a person who is "limited in English proficiency," *patience is a virtue*! Put yourself in their shoes and think how you would feel if the roles were reversed. Here are some easy things you can do to make the conversation easier for both of you.

✓ Speak slowly and distinctly.

✓ Do not use slang expressions.

✓ Get straight to the point! Unnecessary words cloud your meaning.

✓ Speak in a normal tone. Speaking *loudly* doesn't help anyone understand you any better!

✓ Look for cues to meaning in body language and facial expressions. Use gestures of your own to get your point across.

✓ You may not receive good eye contact. Do not interpret the lack of eye contact negatively.

✓ Latinos tend to stand closer to each other than North Americans do when they talk with each other, so your personal space could feel crowded. Stand your ground!

✓ Feel free to use gestures and body language of your own to communicate.

✓ Because of the way languages are learned, it is likely that the person you are talking to understands more of what you are saying, than he is able to verbalize. *So, be careful what you say!* No matter what the language, we always understand the bad words first!

Tips & Tidbits
Throughout your book look for the light bulb you see above. This section will give you helpful hints and cultural information designed to help you learn Spanish more easily.

Beginning Words & Phrases

Your Latino clients will be delighted you are learning to speak *español*. Words like please and thank you show respect and courtesy that will go a long way towards helping you to establish good rapport.

English	Español	Guide
Hi!	¡Hola!	OH-la
How are you?	¿Cómo está?	CO-mo es-TA
Fine	Muy bien.	mooy b-N
So so	Así así	ah-SEE ah-SEE
Bad	Mal	mal
Good morning	Buenos días	boo-WAY-nos D-ahs
Good afternoon	Buenas tardes	boo-WAY-nas TAR-days
Good night	Buenas noches.	boo-WAY-nas NO-chase
Sir or Mister	Señor	sen-YOUR
Mrs. or Ma'am	Señora	sen-YOUR-ah
Miss	Señorita	sen-your- REE-ta
What's your name?	¿Cómo se llama?	CO-mo say YA-ma
My name is ___	Me llamo ____.	may YA-mo
Nice to meet you	Mucho gusto	MOO-cho GOO-stow
Thank you.	Gracias.	GRA-see-ahs
Please	Por favor	pour-fa-VOR
You're welcome.	De nada.	day NA da
The pleasure is mine.	El gusto es mío.	el GOO-stow es ME-oh
I'm sorry.	Lo siento.	low-see-N-toe
Excuse me.	¡Perdón!	pear-DON
We'll see you!	¡Hasta la vista!	AH-sta la VEE-sta
Good-bye	Adiós	ah-dee-OS

13

Spanish Sounds Rápido — What Do I Do Now?

Be honest! One of the reasons you are hesitant to speak Spanish is that it sounds so fast! Naturally, you're afraid you won't understand. Here are some phrases that will help you. Make learning them a priority.

English	Español	Guide
I don't understand.	No comprendo.	no com-**PREN**-doe
Do you understand?	¿Comprende?	com-**PREN**-day
I speak a little Spanish.	Hablo poco español.	**AH**-blow **POE**-co es-pan-**NYOL**
Do you speak English?	¿Habla inglés?	**AH**-bla eng-**LACE**
Repeat, please.	Repita, por favor.	ray-**PETE**-ah pour fa-**VOR**
I'm studying Spanish.	Estudio español.	es-**TOO**-d-oh es-pan-**NYOL**
Write it, please	Escribe, por favor.	es-**SCREE**-bay pour fa-**VOR**
Speak more slowly, please.	Habla más despacio, por favor.	**AH**-bla mas des-**PA**-see-oh pour fa-**VOR**
Thanks for your patience.	Gracias por su paciencia.	**GRA**-see-ahs pour sue pa-see-**N**-see-ah
How do you say it in Spanish?	¿Cómo se dice en español?	**CO**-mo say **DEE**-say n es-pan-**NYOL**
Where are you from?	¿De dónde es?	day **DON**-day es
May I help you?	¿Puedo servirle?	pooh-**A**-doe ser-**VEER**-lay

**Note: Verbs in this section are given in present tense.

The key here is not to pánico. Your Spanish-speaking client is having just as much trouble understanding you, as you are having understanding them! Hang in there! Between the two of you, *comunicación* will begin to take place.

Para Practicar

Practice Conversation I

USTED (YOU):	Good morning, Sir.
SR.GARCÍA	Good morning. How are you?
USTED	Fine, thanks. How are you?
SR. GARCÍA	OK, thanks.

Practice Conversation II

USTED: May I help you? My name is _____.
   I speak a little Spanish. What's your name?

SRA. GARCÍA: My name is Carla García-Hernandez. I speak a little English.

USTED: Nice to meet you.

SRA. GARCÍA: Yes, nice to meet you.

Using phrases found on pages 14-15, practice the following.

✓ A greeting of your choice.

✓ My name is _____.

✓ I speak a little Spanish.

✓ Do you speak English?

✓ Speak more slowly, please.

✓ Thank you.

¿Cuál Es Su Nombre Completo?
What Is Your <u>Complete</u> Name?

Hispanic Names Have Four Parts

First Name Primer Nombre	Middle Name Segundo Nombre	Father's Surname Apellido Paterno	Mother's Surname Apellido Materno
Carlos	Jesús	Santana	Rodríguez
Poncho	Luis	Villa	García
Carmen	Elena	Miranda	Rivera

Start with: Señor, Señora,   or   Señorita

Use Both Names Or Only The Father's Last Name

Sr. Santana   Sr. Villa   Sra. Miranda

When a Woman Marries

She <u>keeps</u> her father's **Apellido Paterno**, and she <u>drops</u> her **Apellido Materno**
In place of her **Apellido Materno** is her husband's **Apellido Paterno**

Children Have The Apellido Paterno of Both Father and Mother

*If Carlos Santana married Carmen Miranda Rivera,
what would her name be after the marriage? What's the complete name
of their child?*

José Carlos ???? ?????

Answer: 1. Carmen Miranda-Santana   2. José Carlos Santana Miranda

16

Spanish Nouns
Can words *really* have a gender?

¡Sí! Spanish belongs to the "romance" language family. It doesn't have anything to do with love, but it has a lot to do with the Romans. In ancient times, people had the same trouble learning languages that they do today—except that there were no cassette tapes, CDs, PDAs or very many foreign language teachers. In those days, there weren't many schools for that matter! Consequently, most people were on their own when it came to learning another language.

To help the difficult process along, words were placed into categories based upon how they sounded. It organized the material and made it easier to learn. Old world languages had categories that were often described as "masculine," "feminine," or even "neuter." From these descriptions, people began talking about words in terms of their gender. Even though the word "gender" is misleading, the tendency to group words by sound helped people learn new languages more quickly.

Because Spanish evolved from Latin, it has maintained two category divisions for thousands of years. The categories are called masculine and feminine. Even though Spanish can and will evolve, the concept of categories in *español* is not likely to change.

Here are the most important points to remember about nouns and their categories:

> **NOUN**
>
> A person, place or thing

1. Usually, the words are grouped by how they sound, not by what they mean. There will always be a few exceptions!

2. Languages are a lot like the people who use them: They don't always follow the rules!

3. If the Spanish noun is referring to a person, the letter will often indicate the sex of that individual. For example: a doctor, who is a man, is a "*doctor*," while a woman, who is a doctor, is a "*doctora*."

4. Words in the "masculine" category usually end with the letter "O".

17

5. Words in the "feminine" category usually end with the letter "A".

6. El, la, los and las are very important words. They all mean "the". They are the clues you need to tell you a word's category.

El (masculine category – singular)   El niño, El muchacho

Los (masculine category – plural)   Los niños, Los muchachos

La (feminine category – singular)   La niña, La muchacha

Las (feminine category – plural)   Las niñas, Las muchachas

A Word about Adjectives

Describing things in Spanish can present problems for English speakers. There are several reasons why using adjectives may give us trouble. First, there is the position of the adjective in relation to the noun. In English, descriptive words go in front of the noun like "white cat," for example. In Spanish, the noun is the most important element, so it comes first. White cat is *un gato blanco*. It is the opposite of our word order. However, it gets more complicated because there are a few basic adjectives which show size or quantity that are placed in front of the noun, just like English. These include words like large (*grande*) and small (*pequeño*), along with numbers. For example: a large white cat is *un grande gato blanco*.

Second, since Spanish nouns are divided into masculine and feminine categories, the adjective must match its noun by category. This means that from time to time you will need to match the letter at the end of the adjective and make it the same letter that is at the end of the noun. You must also match the adjective to the noun by number (singular or plural). This matching sound feature of Spanish is one of the main reasons it has such a musical sound.

Here is an example:
One large white house =   *Una grande casa blanca*
Six large white houses =   *Seis grandes casas blancas*

ADJECTIVE: Describes a noun

Common Adjectives — Adjetivos Comunes

These common adjectives are shown as you would find them in a Spanish dictionary. As written, use them with singular words in the masculine category, and place them behind the noun. Change the "o" at the end to an "a" to make them match up with words in the feminine category. Don't forget to add an "s" at the end for plural words.

English	Español	English	Español
Good	Bueno	Bad	Malo
Better	Mejor	Worse	Peor
Big	Grande	Small	Pequeño
Clean	Limpio	Dirty	Sucio
Hot	Caliente	Cold	Frío
Safe	Seguro	Dangerous	Peligroso
Easy	Fácil	Difficult	Difícil
Full	Lleno	Empty	Vacío
Fast	Rápido	Slow	Lento
New	Nuevo	Old	Viejo
Pretty	Bonito	Ugly	Feo
Quiet	Tranquilo	Restless	Inquieto
Tall	Alto	Short	Bajo
Well	Bien	Sick	Enfermo
Strong	Fuerte	Weak	Débil

Tips & Tidbits
Remember that learning the noun is the most important thing, not which category or gender it is! Words like "el" or "la" only mean "the." They don't give any clues to what you are trying to say. Learning the fine points of grammar can wait until you become a master of communications using Survival Spanish.

The Essentials of Spanish Verbs

There are basically three types of regular verbs in Spanish. The last two letters on the end of the verb determines how it is to be treated. Listed below are the three most common types of regular verb endings.

- ✓ **AR** – Hablar: To speak
- ✓ **ER** – Comprender: To understand
- ✓ **IR** – Escribir: To write

In Survival Spanish, we focus on speaking about ourselves and talking to another person. That's the most common type of "one-on-one" communication.

When you need to say I speak, I understand, or I live, change the last two letters of the verb to an "O".

- ✓ Hablo
- ✓ Comprendo
- ✓ Escribo

When asking a question, such as do you speak, do you understand, or do you live, change the ending to an "a" or an "e". *The change in letter indicates that you are speaking to someone else.*

- ✓ Habla
- ✓ Comprende
- ✓ Escribe

To make a sentence negative, simply put "no" in front of the verb.

- ✓ No hablo
- ✓ No comprendo
- ✓ No escribo

VERB: Shows action or state of being

¡Acción!

There are so many English friendly *acción* words in the Spanish "AR" verb family. Many of them bear a strong resemblance to English verbs—most of them share a simple, regular nature. They are a very important asset in on-the-job communication. We picked a few of our favorites to get you started. Look closely at the list on the next page. On it you will recognize many comforting similarities between our languages that are practical too! Changing one letter will really expand your conversational skills.

In on-the-job conversations, people tend to use "I" and "you" to start many sentences. Of all the pronouns, these two are the most powerful and will work the best for you. That's where we'll start.

Here's an important difference between our languages. In English, the use of pronouns is essential because most of our verbs tend to end the same way. For example, with I speak and you speak; the verb "speak" remains the same. In English, our pronouns make all the difference. Spanish is different in this aspect. Spanish-speaking people are listening for the letters on the end of the verb. That's what indicates who or what is being talked about in Spanish. Each ending is different. The end of the Spanish verb is much more important than the beginning. The ending of the verb tells the Spanish-speaking person who or what is being discussed. In most cases when people speak Spanish, you might not hear a pronoun. It's not necessary for precise meaning. That's a big reason why Spanish might sound a little fast to you:

Pronouns, which are important in English, are routinely eliminated in Spanish!

Try this: Treat the verbs in the "AR" family as you would "to speak" or "hablar." End the verb with an "o" when you're talking about yourself; "hablo" or "I speak". Change the verb ending from an "o" to an "a" for "habla" or "you speak." Use this form when you're talking to someone else.

English	Español	Guide
I need	Necesito	nay-say-SEE-toe
You need	Necesita	nay-say-SEE-ta

The Sweet Sixteen Verbs

This list contains sixteen of the most commonly used regular verbs in the "AR" verb family. Since they are so practical for use on the job, begin learning them and using them first.

English	Español	Guide
To ask	Preguntar	prey-goon-**TAR**
To bother	Molestar	mo-les-**TAR**
To call	Llamar	ya-**MAR**
To investigate	Investigar	een-vest-t-**GAR**
To cooperate	Cooperar	co-op-air-**RAR**
To forget	Olvidar	ohl-v-**DAR**
To fill out	Llenar	yea-**NAR**
To need	Necesitar	nay-say-see-**TAR**
To observe	Observar	ob-ser-**VAR**
To pay	Pagar	pa-**GAR**
To prepare	Preparar	pray-pa-**RAR**
To return	Regresar	ray-grey-**SAR**
To verify	Verificar	ver-ree-fee-**CAR**
To use	Usar	oo-**SAR**
To earn	Ganar	Ga-**NAR**
To work	Trabajar	tra-baa-**HAR**

**Note: To make a sentence negative, say no in front of the verb.
   Example: I don't need. **No necesito.** You don't need **No necesita.**

Which verbs in the Sweet 16 do you use most often? List your top five:

1. _____

2. _____

3. _____

4. _____

5. _____

Tú and Usted

In español there are two words for "you": Usted and tú.

Usted is for adults, strangers, and acquaintances.
Tú is for children and close friends.

When using usted, your verb will end in the letter "a."

When using tú, your verb should end with "as."

Now take your top five and change the AR ending to an "a" to indicate you are talking to someone else. Example: habla meaning you speak.

1. _____

2. _____

3. _____

4. _____

5. _____

¡Necesito una breaka!
¿Y usted?

23

Irregular Verbs: The Big Five

Now that you have had the opportunity to learn about the tremendous number of verbs that follow regular patterns in Spanish, it's time to take a look at others that don't follow the rules. They are unpredictable, but they are very important. In fact, they reflect some of man's oldest concepts. That's why they tend to be irregular. These words were in use long before language rules and patterns were set. There are two verbs in Spanish that mean "to be." The others are: to have, to make and to go. Because they don't follow the rules, you will need to memorize them, but that should be easy because you will use and hear them often.

In English, the "to be" verb is I am, you are, he is, etc. The Spanish version is **ser** and **estar**. *Ser* is used to express permanent things like your nationality or profession. *Estar* is used when talking about location or conditions that change like a person's health.

SER		ESTAR	
Yo **soy**	Nosotros **somos**	Yo **estoy**	Nosotros **estamos**
Tú **eres**		Tú **estás**	
Él **es**	Ellos **son**	Él **está**	Ellos **están**
Ella **es**	Ellas **son**	Ella **está**	Ellas **están**
Usted **es**	Ustedes **son**	Usted **está**	Ustedes **están**

The verb *"to have"* in Spanish is *muy importante*. In English, we say that we are hot, cold, hungry, thirsty, right, wrong, or sleepy, but in Spanish those are conditions that you have. Some of those expressions mean something totally different than you expected if you get the verbs confused, so be careful!

TENER

Yo **tengo**	Nosotros **tenemos**
Tú **tienes**	
Él **tiene**	Ellos **tienen**
Ella **tiene**	Ellas **tienen**
Usted **tiene**	Ustedes **tienen**

In Spanish, the verb that means, *"to do"* also means, *"to make."* It's not unusual for one verb to have multiple meanings. There are many expressions that require the use of this verb, but you will use it most when you talk about the weather. That's a safe subject and one that everyone, the world over, discusses! **¿Qué tiempo hace?** What's the weather? **Hace frío.** (It's cold.) **Hace sol.** (It's sunny). **Hace calor.** (It's hot) **Hace viento** (It's windy.). Here are two exceptions: **Está lloviendo** (It's raining.) and **Está nevando.** (It's snowing.)

HACER

Yo **hago**	Nosotros **hacemos**
Tú **haces**	
Él **hace**	Ellos **hacen**
Ella **hace**	Ellas **hacen**
Usted **hace**	Ustedes **hacen**

The last of the big five is perhaps the easiest to use. It's the verb that means, *"to go"*. In Spanish, that's **ir**. It's pronounced like the English word ear. Both in English and in Spanish, we use parts of it to make the future tense, in other words, to talk about things that we are going to do. Look at the parts of *ir*. Then look back at the parts of the verb *ser*. Do you see any similarities?

IR

Yo **voy**	Nosotros **vamos**
Tú **vas**	
Él **va**	Ellos **van**
Ella **va**	Ellas **van**
Usted **va**	Ustedes **van**

When you want to say something that you are going to do, start with I'm going or *voy*. Next, insert the word *"a"* and the basic verb that states what it is that you're going to do. Try it! It's easy. Here are some examples.

Voy a visitar a mi familia.	I am going to visit my family.
Voy a organizar el proyecto.	I am going to organize the project.
Mario va a comprar las plantas.	Mario is going to buy the plants.

**Note: The whole concept of irregular verbs can be quite daunting. Don't let it defeat you! We have many irregular verbs in English. Every language has them. The only way to master them is to use them. Make them your own! Try writing different parts of a verb on your desk calendar. That way, it will be there in front of you every time you look down. When you see it, say it to yourself. Then, you'll have it conquered in no time.

Are You Hungry? — ¿Tiene Hambre?

Using the right verb at the right time is very important. The following common expressions in Spanish require the use of *tener*. These are phrases you must learn, even though the translation will feel strange to you. *Remember our English idioms often sound very strange to non-native speakers.*

As a rule, *tener* is used to describe physical conditions. In English we use the verb *to be* instead.

TENER: *To have* **TENGO**: *I have* **TIENE**: *You have*

English	Español	Guide
Hot	Calor	ca-**LORE**
Hungry	Hambre	**AM**-bray
Cold	Frío.	**FREE**-oh
Ashamed	Vergüenza	ver-goo-**N**-sa
In pain.	Dolor	doe-**LORE**
Afraid of	Miedo de	me-**A**-doe day
Right	Razón	rah-**SEWN**
Thirsty	Sed	said
Sleepy	Sueño	soo-**WAYNE**-nyo
xx years old	*xx* años	xx **AHN**-nyos

What's The Weather? — ¿Qué Tiempo Hace?

No matter what the culture is a general topic for discussion is always the weather. Discussing the weather in Spanish requires a different verb from the one used in English. If you say to your host, "*Está frío*," he or she would think that you were talking about something you had touched. In Spanish, use the verb **hacer** which means to do or to make to describe the weather. It's one of the big five irregulars.

English	Español	Guide
What's the weather?	¿Qué tiempo hace?	kay t-M-po AH-say
To be nice weather	Hace buen tiempo	AH-say boo-WAYNE t-M-po
To be hot	Hace calor	AH-say ca-LORE
To be cool	Hace fresco	AH-say FRES-co
To be sunny	Hace sol	AH-say sol
To be windy	Hace viento	AH-say v-N-toe
To be cold	Hace frío	AH-say FREE-oh
Rain	Lluvia	U-v-ah
To rain.	Llover	YO-ver

Tips & Tidbits

In America we use the Fahrenheit scale for measuring the temperature. Latin Americans countries use the Celsius scale. Do you know what the difference is? Here's a simple example: 0 degrees Celsius is 32 degrees Fahrenheit.

27

Special Uses of Ser and Estar

The verbs *ser* and *estar* both mean the same thing in English: *to be,* but *how can two verbs mean the same thing?* It's because *ser* and *estar* are used in very different ways. Spanish sees these two verbs differently and uses them in very precise ways. Listed below are some simple guidelines on their usage:

Common Uses of Ser

A. **To express an permanent quality or characteristic**

La puerta es de madera.	The door is made of wood.
El hospital es enorme.	The hospital is enormous.
Los doctores son importantes.	Doctors are important.

B. **To describe or identify**

Mi amigo es médico.	My friend is a doctor.
El estudiante es alto.	The student is tall.

C. **To indicate nationality**

Pedro es mexicano.	Pedro is Mexican.
La historia es de Argentina.	The story is from Argentina.

D. **To express ownership**

Este es mi auto.	This is my car.
Este es mi libro.	This is my book.

E. **To express time and dates**

¿Qué hora es?	What time is it?
Hoy es el nueve de junio.	Today is the 9th of June.

F. **With impersonal expressions.**

Es importante estudiar.	It's important to study.
Es necesario leer.	It's necessary to read.

Common Uses of Estar

A. **To express location**

Estoy en la oficina.	I am in the office.
Charlotte está en Carolina del Norte.	Charlotte is in North Carolina.
El baño está en el segundo piso.	The bathroom is on the 2nd floor.

B. **To indicate someone's health**

Mi esposa está enferma.	My wife is sick.
¿Cómo está usted?	How are you?

C. **Estar is also used as a helping verb**

Estoy hablando.	I am speaking.
Carmen está trabajando.	Carmen is working.
Julio está regresando mañana.	Julio is returning tomorrow.

Tips & Tidbits

Notice from the examples that *ser* is used more frequently than *estar*. Even though the usage of *ser* and *estar* seems complicated in the beginning, both verbs are used so frequently in conversation that you will become comfortable using them quickly. Begin with the "I" or "yo" form of each verb. Next, tackle the "you" or "usted" form. You will use those two forms of the verb's conjugation much more than the other parts of it.

The Numbers — Los Números

When you are talking to a native speaker and you are discussing anything involving numbers, keep the following important information in mind:

1. Most people say numbers **extremely** fast! Don't hesitate to ask for a number to be said more slowly or to be repeated. Review the chapter called **Spanish Sounds Rápido — What Do I Do Now?**

2. When native speakers are saying phone numbers, many pair the numbers together instead of saying them as single digits.

3. If you are expressing a date which contains the year, often a native speaker will say the complete number. For example: 1962 will be said "one thousand nine hundred sixty and two" or "**mil novecientos sesenta y dos.**" If you wish, it is also correct to pair the numbers as "nineteen sixty-two" or "diez y nueve sesenta y dos."

Number	Español	Guide
0	Cero	SAY-row
1	Uno	OO-no
2	Dos	dose
3	Tres	trays
4	Cuatro	coo-AH-trow
5	Cinco	SINK-oh
6	Seis	SAY-ees
7	Siete	see-A-tay
8	Ocho	OH-cho
9	Nueve	new-A-vay

Number	Español	Guide
10	Diez	d-**ACE**
11	Once	**ON**-say
12	Doce	**DOSE**-a
13	Trece	**TRAY**-say
14	Catorce	ca-**TOR**-say
15	Quince	**KEEN**-say
16	Diez y seis	d- **ACE** e **SAY**-ees
17	Diez y siete	d- **ACE** e see-**ATE**-tay
18	Diez y ocho	d- **ACE** e **OH**-cho
19	Diez y nueve	d- **ACE** e new-**A**-vay
20	Veinte	**VAIN**-tay
21	Veinte y uno	**VAIN**-tay e **OO**-no
22	Veinte y dos	**VAIN**-tay e dose
23	Veinte y tres	**VAIN**-tay e trays
24	Veinte y cuatro	**VAIN**-tay e coo-**AH**-trow
25	Veinte y cinco	**VAIN**-tay e **SINK**-oh
26	Veinte y seis	**VAIN**-tay e **SAY**-ees
27	Veinte y siete	**VAIN**-tay e see-**A**-tay
28	Veinte y ocho	**VAIN**-tay e **OH**-cho -
29	Veinte y nueve	**VAIN**-tay e new-**A**-vay
30	Treinta	**TRAIN**-ta

Number	Español	Guide
40	Cuarenta	kwah-**RAIN**-ta
50	Cincuenta	seen-**KWAIN**-ta
60	Sesenta	say-**SAIN**-ta
70	Setenta	say-**TAIN**-ta
80	Ochenta	oh-**CHAIN**-ta
90	Noventa	no-**VAIN**-ta
100	Cien	see-**IN**
200	Doscientos	dose-see-**N**-tos
300	Trescientos	tray-see-**N**-tos
400	Cuatrocientos	coo-**AH**-troh-see-**N**-tos
500	Quinientos	keen-e-**N**-tos
600	Seiscientos	**SAY**-ees-see-**N**-tos
700	Setecientos	**SAY**-tay-see-**N**-tos
800	Ochocientos	**OH**-choh-see-**N**-tos
900	Novecientos	**NO**-vay-see-**N**-tos
1,000	Mil	meal

Para Practicar

1. Practice your home, office and cell phone number.

2. Practice saying the number for the date each day.

3. Practice saying the numbers on the license plates of cars in front of you when you are stopped in traffic.

4. Practice saying the numbers for highways near your home or office.

The Days of the Week and Months of the Year

Los Días de la Semana

English	Español	Guide
Monday	lunes	LOON-ace
Tuesday	martes	MAR-tays
Wednesday	miércoles	me-AIR-co-lace
Thursday	jueves	who-WAVE-ace
Friday	viernes	v-AIR-nace
Saturday	sábado	SAH-ba-doe
Sunday	domingo	doe-MING-go

When expressing a date in Spanish, give the number of the day first. Follow the day with the month. Use this format: El (date) de (month).

Los Meses del Año

English	Español	Guide
January	enero	n-NAY-row
February	febrero	fay-BRAY-row
March	marzo	MAR-so
April	abril	ah-BRILL
May	mayo	MY-oh
June	junio	WHO-knee-oh
July	julio	WHO-lee-oh
August	agosto	ah-GOS-toe
September	septiembre	sep-tee-EM-bray
October	octubre	oc-TOO-bray
November	noviembre	no-v-EM-bray
December	diciembre	d-see-EM-bray

Your appointment is (day of the week) el (number) de (month).
Su cita es lunes, el 11 de octubre.

33

Practicing Numbers & Dates

Practice these important items by using numbers, days of the week, and months of the year:

✓ Your social security number

✓ Your driver's license number

✓ The numbers in your address

✓ Your zip code

✓ Your phone number

✓ Your birth date

✓ Your children's birth dates

✓ The dates of holidays

✓ License tags of the cars in front of you, when you are stopped in traffic.

Combine the Spanish alphabet with this exercise.

✓ Phone numbers you see on billboards

✓ Numbers found on street signs

✓ Phone numbers when you dial them at work or at home

✓ The appointments on your personal calendar

✓ Your wedding anniversary

✓ The dates of all your Spanish classes or practice sessions

What Time Is It? — ¿Qué Hora Es?

The concept of time is something that varies from culture to culture. Many countries put less emphasis on being on time for certain things than Americans do. In Latino culture one lives for the present. It can be especially true in one's personal life; however, on the job everyone knows the value of *puntualidad*. *¡Es muy importante!*

Learning to tell time is another good way to put your numbers in Spanish to good use *¿Qué hora es?* means *what time is it?*

It's one o'clock.	Es la una.
It's two o'clock.	Son las dos.
It's 3:30.	Son las tres y media.
It's 5:45.	Son las seis menos quince.

Use the phrases *de la mañana* to indicate morning and *de la tarde* to indicate afternoon. Also midnight is *medianoche*. Noon is *mediodía*.

To find out at what time something takes place ask: *¿A qué hora...?*

| ¿A qué hora es la reunión? | What time is the meeting? |
| ¿A qué hora termina? | What time do you finish? |

Spanish speakers sometimes use the 24-hour clock for departures and arrivals of trains and flights, etc.

12:05	las doce cero cinco
17.52	las diez y siete cincuenta y dos
23.10	las veinte y tres diez
07.15	las siete quince

Para Practicar

Using the word for meeting "la reunion," say that your meeting takes place on the hour throughout your workday. La reunión es a las ocho.

Scheduling an Appointment

When you need to schedule an appointment, this form will come in very handy for you. In *español* an appointment is called a *cita* (SEE-ta). List the name of the individual that the appointment is with first. Then circle the day of the week and add the number for the day. Finally, circle the month and add the time. The phrase at the bottom of this form simply asks the individual to arrive ten minutes early for the appointment.

Usted tiene una cita importante con _____.

La cita es   lunes   el _____ de   enero   a las _____.

                martes   febrero

                miércolcs   marzo

                jueves   abril

                viernes   mayo

junio

julio

agosto

septiembre

octubre

noviembre

diciembre

**Favor de llegar 10 minutos antes del tiempo de su cita. ¡Gracias!
Please arrive 10 minutes before the time of your appointment. Thank you.

The Questions Everyone Should Know

English	Español	Guide
Who?	¿Quién?	key-N
What?	¿Qué?	kay
Which?	¿Cuál?	coo-ALL
When?	¿Cuándo?	KWAN-doe
Where?	¿Dónde?	DON-day
Why?	¿Por qué?	pour KAY
How?	¿Cómo?	CO-mo
What's happening?	¿Qué pasa?	kay PA-sa
How much?	¿Cuánto?	KWAN-toe
How many?	¿Cuántos?	KWAN-toes

When you ask a question in Spanish, it will take on the same form as a question does in English. Start with the question word that asks the information you need. Follow the question word with a verb, and give your voice an upward inflection.

In Spanish you can also make a question by ending your sentence with *¿no?* Here's an example: *Cancún está en México, ¿no?* When you end a sentence with "no" like this, it takes on the meaning of "isn't it."

The Most Common Questions

How are you?   ¿Cómo está?

How much does it cost?   ¿Cuánto cuesta?

Where are you from?   ¿De dónde es?

To make the Spanish upside down question mark or the upside down exclamation mark refer, to the chapter called "Typing in Spanish on Your Computer."

Getting the Información

Listed below are common phrases that are used to fill out almost any questionnaire. It seems like most forms always ask for much of the same information in almost the same order. By learning a few simple phrases, you can use this format to your advantage.

There are so many times when we need to ask for very basic information. Most of these questions begin with the words *"what is your."* When you are asking this type of question, remember that it's not always necessary to make a complete sentence to have good communication. The information you are asking for is much more important than the phrase "what is your"? As long as you remember to make what you say *sound* like a question by giving your voice an *upward* inflection, people will interpret what you've said *as* a question.

Use the form on the following page. It asks for very basic information. To help you practice, work with a partner. Make up new information about yourself and complete the form. At each practice session one of you will ask the questions and the other will give the answers to fill in the information requested. This is a great practice exercise, because when you think about it, most of the time the questions you ask will be the same, but the answers you get will always be different!

What's your. . .   ¿Cuál es su. . .
coo-ALL es sue

English	Español	Guide
Full name	Nombre completo	NOM-bray com-PLAY-toe
First name	Primer nombre	pre-MARE NOM-bray
Middle name	Segundo nombre	say-GOON-doe NOM-bray
Last name (surname)	Apellido	ah-pay-YE-doe
Paternal surname	Apellido paterno	ah-pay-YE-doe pa-TER-no

English	Español	Guide
Maternal surname	Apellido materno	ah-pay-**YE**-doe ma-**TER**-no
Address	Dirección	d-wreck-see-**ON**
Apartment number	Número de apartamento	**NEW**-may-row day ah-par-ta-**MEN**-toe
Age	Edad	a-**DAD**
Date of birth	Fecha de nacimiento	**FAY**-cha day na-see-me-**N**-toe
Nationality	Nacionalidad	na-see-on-nal-e-**DAD**
Place of birth	Lugar de nacimiento	loo-**GAR** day na-see-me-**N**-toe
Place of employment	Lugar de empleo	loo-**GAR** day m-**PLAY**-oh
Occupation	Ocupación	oh-coo-pa-see-**ON**
Home telephone number	Número de teléfono de su casa	**NEW**-may-row day tay-**LAY**-fo-no day sue **CA**-sa
Work telephone number	Número de teléfono de su empleo	**NEW**-may-row day tay-**LAY**-fo-no day sue m-**PLAY**-oh
Marital status	Estado civil	es-**TA**-doe see-**VEAL**
Married	Casado (a)	ca-**SA**-doe
Single	Soltero (a)	soul-**TAY**-row
Divorced	Divorciado (a)	d-vor-see-**AH**-doe
Widow	Viudo (a)	v-**OO**-doe
Separated	Separado (a)	sep-pa-**RAH**-doe
Driver's license number	Número de licencia	**NEW**-may-row day lee-**SEN**-see-ah
Social security number	Número de seguro social	**NEW**-may-row day say-**GOO**-row sew-see-**AL**

Información Básica
Imprima por favor

Fecha: _____

                                               Mes   Día   Año

Sr.

Sra.

Srta._____

    Primer Nombre   Segundo Nombre   Apellido Paterno   Apellido Materno (Esposo)

Dirección:_____

                                Calle

_____

Ciudad   *Estado*   *Zona postal*

Teléfono: Casa_____   Empleo_____

          Cel_____   Fax _____

Correo electrónico

_____

Número de seguro social: _____-_____-_____

Fecha de nacimiento   _____

                    Mes   Día   Año

Número de la licencia: _____

Ocupación: _____

Lugar de empleo_____

Estado civil: ☐ Casado (a)   ☐ Divorciado (a)

                ☐ Soltero (a)   ☐ Separado (a)

                ☐ Viudo (a)

Nombre de esposo:_____

      Primer Nombre Segundo Nombre   Apellido Paterno Apellido Materno

Nombre de esposa: _____

       Primer Nombre Segundo Nombre Apellido Paterno Apellido Materno/Esposo

En caso de emergencia:_____Teléfono: _____

Firma: _____ Fecha: _____

See back of book for English translation of the basic information form.

Public Assistance — Asistencia Pública

The US provides various government funded assistance programs for those in need. In order to qualify for these programs, an individual must show proof of need and meet other eligibility requirements. Most Latin American countries have no social programs at all—or they are very limited. As a result, many Latinos are not aware that there are programs to help them or they do not know how to access them.

Three major programs in the United States that provide financial assistance are: Medicaid, Supplemental Security Income (SSI), and Aid to Families with Dependent Children (AFDC). The Spanish terms for these programs are almost impossible to translate literally, because these programs do not exist outside the United States. Since most Spanish-speaking clients will refer to the these programs using the English term or the same acronym that we use, that will make the complicated job of determining eligibility a bit easier.

The application process for benefits can be lengthy and complicated. In order to apply, a client must visit a county or city social services office where a social worker is assigned to the case. The case worker interviews the client to determine eligibility. For an individual who is limited in English proficiency, the application process can be stressful and overwhelming. Language barriers can make this difficult procedure even worse. These phrases will help your initial meeting to go more smoothly.

English	Español	Guide
Please sit down.	Favor de sentarse.	fa-**VOR** day sen-**TAR**-say
May I help you?	¿Puedo ayudarle?	poo-**A**-doe eye-you-**DAR**-ley

English	Español	Guide
How do you write your name?	¿Cómo escribe su nombre?	CO-mo es-SCREE-bay sue NOM-bray
Do you need to apply for Aid for Families with Dependent Children (AFDC)?	¿Necesita solicitar AFDC?	nay-say-SEE-ta so-lee-see-TAR ah-F-ay-day-say
Do you need SSI?	¿Necesita solicitar SSI?	nay-say-SEE-ta so-lee-see-TAR s-ay-s-ay-e
Where do you live?	¿Dónde vive?	DON-day V-vay
Is this your current address?	¿Es ésta su dirección actual?	es ES-ta sue d-wreck-see-ON act-too-AL
Are you a US citizen?	¿Es ciudadano (a) de los Estados Unidos?	es see-oo-da-DAHN-oh day los es-TAH-does oo-KNEE-dose
Are you a legal resident?	¿Es residente legal?	es ray-see-DEN-tay lay-GAL
Are you a legal immigrant?	¿Es inmigrante legal?	es een-me-GRAN-tay lay-GAL
You need proof of legal residency or citizenship.	Necesita un comprobante de residencia legal o ciudadanía.	nay-say-SEE-ta oon com-pro-BAHN-tay day ray-see-DEN-see-ah lay-GAL oh see-oo-da-da-KNEE-ah
Do you have the necessary paperwork?	¿Tiene el papeleo necesario?	t-N-a l pa-pell-A-oh nay-say-SAR-ree-oh
Do you have?	¿Tiene?	t-N-a
Identification	Identificación	e-den-t-fee-ca-see-ON
Social security card	Tarjeta de seguro social	tar-HEY-ta day say-GOO-row so-see-AL
Birth certificate	Certificado de nacimiento	cer-t-fee-CA-doe day na-see-me-N-toe

English	Español	Guide
Passport	Pasaporte	pa-sa-**POUR**-tay
License	Licencia	lee-**SEN**-see-ah
Permanent resident card	Tarjeta de residencia permanente	tar-**HEY**-ta day ray-see-**DEN**-see-ah pear-may-**NEN**-tay
Income	Ingreso	een-**GRAY**-so
How much?	¿Cuánto?	coo-**AHN**-toe
I will have to verify this.	Tengo que verificar esto.	**TANG**-go kay ver-ree-fee-**CAR** **ES**-toe
What is your ethnicity?	¿Cuál es su grupo étnico?	coo-**ALL** es sue **GREW**-po **ATE**-knee-co
Have you ever applied for public assistance?	¿Ha solicitado alguna vez asistencia pública?	ah-so-lee-see-**TA**-doe al-**GOO**-na vase ah-sees-**TEN**-see-ah **POO**-blee-ca
You are eligible for Medicaid insurance.	Es elegible para el seguro de Medicaid.	es a-lay-**HE**-blay **PA**-rah l say-**GOO**-row Medicaid
You are eligible for food stamps.	Es elegible para estampillas de comida.	es a-lay-**HE**-blay **PA**-rah es-stam-**P**-yas day co-**ME**-da
At what address do you receive mail?	¿A qué dirección recibe correo?	ah kay d-wreck-see-**ON** ray-**SEE**-bay core-**A**-oh

Para Practicar:
Which of the phrases in this chapter do you use daily? Make a list of these useful phrases and vocabulary words on index cards. Keep those at your desk for a quick, handy reference.

Food Stamps — Estampillas para Alimentos

The federal food stamp program is an important benefit that many families need to provide nutritious food for their families. After you have worked through questions dealing with eligibility, you may need to discuss the food stamp program and explain what items the coupons can be used to purchase. The following vocabulary will help you with all the *básicos.*

English	Español	Guide
With these coupons you can buy	Con estos estampillas puede comprar	con **ES**-toes es-stam-**P**-yas poo-**A**-day com-**PRAR**
Bread	Pan	pahn
Cereal	Cereales	say-ree-**AL**-ace
Fruits	Frutas	**FRU**-tas
Vegetables	Vegitales	vay-he-**TAL**-ace
Greens	Verduras	ver-**DOO**-rahs
Meat	Carne	**CAR**-nay
Fish	Pez	pes
Poultry	Aves	**AH**-vays
Dairy products	Productos lácteos	pro-**DUKE**-toes **LAC**-tay-ohs
You can not buy	No puede comprar	no poo-**A**-day com-**PRAR**
Beer	Cerveza	ser-**VASE**-ah
Wine	Vino	**V**-no
Liquor	Licor	lee-**CORE**
Cigarettes	Cigarillos	see-ga-**REE**-yos
Tobacco	Tabaco	ta-**BA**-co

English	Español	Guide
Pet food	Comida para mascotas	co-ME-da PA-rah mas-CO-tas
Soap	Jabon	ha-BONE
Paper products	Productos de papel	pro-DUKE-toes day pa-PELL
Household supplies	Artículos para la casa	are-T-coo-lows PA-rah la CA-sa
Vitamins	Vitaminas	v-ta-ME-nas
Medicines	Medicamentos	may-d-ca-MEN-toes
Hot foods	Comida caliente	co-ME-da ca-lee-N-tay
Food that is eaten in the store.	Alimentos que se comen en la tienda	al-lee-MEN-toes kay say CO-men in la t-N-da

Remember — Recuerda

English	Español	Guide
Remember	Recuerda	ray-coo-AIR-da
Don't exchange the coupons for cash.	No cambie los cupones por dinero en efectivo.	no CAM-b-a los coo-PON-ace pour d-NAY-row in a-fec-T-vo
You can not use them to pay for a credit account.	No se puede usarlos para pagar una cuenta de crédito.	no say poo-A-day oo-SAR-los PA-rah pa-GAR OO-na coo-WAYNE-ta day CRAY-d-toe

English	Español	Guide
Retailers must not charge taxes on purchases made with food stamps.	Vendedores no deben cobrar impuestos sobre productos comprados con estampillas para alimentos.	ven-day-**DOOR**-ace no **DAY**-ben co-**BRARE** eem-poo-**ACE**-toes **SO**-bray pro-**DUKE**-toes com-**PRA**-dose con eh-stam-**P**-yas **PA**-rah al-lee-**MEN**-toes
With food stamps you can eat a variety of foods.	Con estampillas para alimentos puede comer alimentos más variados.	con eh-stam-**P**-yas **PA**-rah al-lee-**MEN**-toes poo-**A**-day co-**MARE** al-lee-**MEN**-toes mas va-ree-**AH**-dose

In the Grocery Store

To help you in your discussion of food stamps and the importance of eating a varied, healthy diet, learning the words for other items that food stamps can purchase will be helpful to you. Hispanic tastes in foods and beverages are influencing the items we see on supermarket shelves every day. In many Central and South American countries the variety of fresh fruits and vegetables is astounding. Many of the items can be purchased with food stamps.

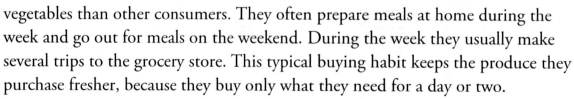

According to several marketing surveys, Latin Americans tend to use more fresh fruits and vegetables than other consumers. They often prepare meals at home during the week and go out for meals on the weekend. During the week they usually make several trips to the grocery store. This typical buying habit keeps the produce they purchase fresher, because they buy only what they need for a day or two.

English	Español	Guide
Beans	Frijoles	free-**HO**-les
Beef	Carne de vaca	**CAR**-nay day **VA**-ca
Beer	Cerveza	ser-**VAY**-sa
Bread	Pan	pahn
Butter	Mantequilla	mahn-tay-**KEY**-ya
Cake mix	Harina preparada para pastel	ah-**REE**-na pre-par-**RAH**-da **PA**-rah pas-**TEL**
Canned goods	Alimentos enlatados	ah-lee-**MEN**-toes n-la-**TA**-dose
Canned vegetables	Vegetales enlatados	vay-he-**TAL**-es n-la-**TA**-dose
Cereal	Cereal	say-ree-**AL**
Cheese	Queso	**KAY**-so
Convenience food	Platos preparados	**PLA**-toes pray-pa-**RA**-does
Cookie	Galleta	ga-**YEA**-ta
Detergent	Detergente	day-ter-**HEN**-tay
Drinks	Bebidas	bay-**B**-dahs
Eggs	Huevos	oo-**WAVE**-ohs
Fish	Pescado	pes-**CA**-does
Flowers	Flores	**FLOOR**-res
Freezer	Congelador	con-hell-ah-**DOOR**
Fruit	Fruta	**FRU**-ta
Ice-cream	Helado	a-**LA**-doe
Juice	Jugo	**WHO**-go
Lard	Manteca	man-**TAKE**-ah
Meat	Carne	**CAR**-nay

English	Español	Guide
Milk	Leche	**LAY**-che
Oil	Aceite	ah-**SAY**-tay
Pasta	Fideo	fee-**DAY**-oh
Poultry	Carne de ave	**CAR**-nay day **AH**-vay
Produce	Productos del campo	pro-**DUKE**-toes del **CAM**-po
Rice	Arroz	ah-**ROS**
Snacks	Aperitivos	ah-pear-ree-**T**-vos
Soup	Sopa	**SO**-pa
Vegetables	Vegetales	vay-he-**TAL**-es
Wine	Vino	**V**-no

Para Practicar

The Alvarez family is preparing to go grocery shopping. Make a list of items that they can use their food stamps to purchase.

1. _____

2. _____

3. _____

4. _____

Tips & Tidbits
Hispanics tend to buy more fresh produce and meats than other segments of the population, and they tend to eat out less frequently.

Social Services —Servicios Sociales

When you begin organizing a long list of vocabulary like this basic list of common words used in social services offices, it's easy to get overwhelmed. It's natural to be unsure about where you should start but — without having a strategy for success, you could become discouraged. *Por favor*, hang in there! Here are some practical tips to help you prioritize the process. First, only scan the words on the list to see if there any that you recognize. Second, focus on any words that have a strong relationship or are *cognates* to English words. Now, go back through the *lista* and begin by marking the ten words that you would like to learn first. They should be the words from the list that are the ones you will use the most. *Always start learning your priority vocabulary first.* After you are confident that you have learned your first ten words, mark ten more.

Now you are ready to concentrate on your "B" list. Don't take on another set of vocabulary until you have learned the one you have in progress. With languages it's better to learn slowly. If you do, you'll remember your words longer and be able to recall them faster. The real secret to learning new words in *español* is organization. Breaking the material down into small "bites" will make a world of *diferencia*!

English	Español	Guide
Accusation	Denuncia	day-**NUN**-see-ah
Address	Dirección	dee-wreck-see-**ON**
Appointment	Cita	**SEE**-tah
Bilingual	Bilingüe	bee-**LEN**-gway
Bill	Cuenta	coo-**N**-tah
Birth certificate	Certificado de nacimiento	ser-tee-fee-**CA**-doe day nah-see-me-**N**-toe
Case	Caso	**CA**-so

English	Español	Guide
Child abuse	Abuso de niños Maltrato de niños	ah-**BOO**-so day-**NEEN**-nyos mal-tra-toe day **NEEN**-nyos
Child protective services	Sección Protectora de Niños	sec-see-**ON** pro-tec-**TOR**-ah day **NEEN**-nyos
Children	Niños	**NEEN**-nyos
Clinic	Clínica	**CLEN**-knee-ka
Doctor	Doctor	doc-**TOR**
Eligible	Elegible	a-lay-**HE**-blay
Factory	Factoría	fac-tor-**REE**-ah
Family	Familia	fa-**MEE**-lee-ah
Financial	Financiero	fee-nahn-see-**AIR**-o
Food	Comida	ko-**MEE**-dah
Food stamps	Estampillas para alimentos Cupones de comida	es-stamp-**EE**-yas **PAH**-ra ah-lee-**MEN**-toes coo-**PON**-es day co-**MEE**-da
Form	Forma	**FOR**-ma
Green card *(slang)* Permanent resident card	Tarjeta verde *(slang)* Tarjeta de residencia permanente	tar-**HEY**-ta **VER**-day tar-**HEY**-ta day ray-see-**DEN**-see-ah pear-me-**N**-tay
Head of household	Jefe de la familia	**HEY**-fay day la fa-**ME**-lee-ah

English	Español	Guide
Health department	Departamento de Salud	day-par-ta-MEN-toe day sa-LEWD
Help	Ayuda	ay-YOU-da
Homeless	Sin hogar	seen oh-GAR
Hospital	Hospital	os-pee-TAL
Housewife	Ama de casa	AH-ma day CA-sa
Husband	Esposo	es-PO-so
Immigration	Inmigración	n-me-grah-see-ON
Income	Entrada	n-TRA-da
Information	Información	n-for-ma-see-ON
Job	Empleo	em-PLAY-oh
Legal	Legal	lay-GAL
Lie	Mentira	men-TEAR-ah
Mail	Correo	Core-RAY-oh
Marriage license	Certificado de matrimonio	ser-t-fee-KAH-doe day ma-tree-MON-knee-oh
Medicaid	El programa federal de ayuda médica	l pro-GRAH-ma fe-day-RAL day ah-YOU-da MAY-d-ka
Medical Insurance	Seguro médico	say-GOO-row MAY-d-ka
Money	Dinero	d-NAY-row
Mortgage	Hipoteca	e-po-TAY-ka
PO box	Apartado postal	ah-par-TA-doe pos-TAL
Program	Programa	pro-GRA-ma

English	Español	Guide
Receipt	Recibo	ray-SEE-bo
Receptionist	Recepcionista	ray-cep-see-on-EES-ta
Service	Servicio	ser-V-see-oh
Social security	Seguro social	say-GOO-row so-see-AL
Social Security card	Tarjeta de seguro social	tar-HEY-ta day say-GOO-row so-see-AL
Social worker	Trabajador(a) social	tra-ba-ha-DOOR so-see-AL
Subsidy	Subsidio	sub-SEE-d-o
To advise	Avisar	ah-v-CZAR
To earn	Ganar	gah-NAR
To examine	Examinar	x-ah-me-NAR
To fill out	Llenar	yea-NAR
To investigate	Investigar	n-ves-tee-GAR
To mistreat	Maltratar	mal-tray-TAR
To need	Necesitar	nay-say-see-TAR
To pay	Pagar	Pa-GAR
Work (n)	Trabajo	tra-BA-ho
Work full time	Trabajar tiempo completo	tra-ba-HAR t-M-po com-PLAY-toe
Work part-time	Trabajar parcial tiempo	tra-ba-HAR par-see-YAL tee-M-po
Work permit	Permiso de trabajo	per-MEE-so day tra-ba-HO

52

The Family — La Familia

Putting our families first is something all Americans have in common. It is especially true for Latinos. For them, family values are extremely important. No sacrifice is too great if it helps the family. Children are considered to be precious gifts. Wives, mothers, and grandmothers are highly respected. Remember that the maternal side of the family is so important that traditionally Hispanics carry their mother's surname or *materno apellido* as a part of their complete name. If you have forgotten the four important parts of a Latino's name, please review the chapter called *"Cuál es su nombre completo."*

You are certainly going to hear about members of the family from your Hispanic clients. It's something all of us like to talk about!

English	Español	Guide
Aunt	Tía	T-ah
Uncle	Tío	T-oh
Brother	Hermano	air-MAN-oh
Sister	Hermana	air-MAN-ah
Brother-in-law	Cuñado	coon-YA-doe
Sister-in-law	Cuñada	coon-YA-da
Child	Niño *(m)*	KNEE-nyo
	Niña *(f)*	KNEE-nya
Cousin	Primo *(m)*	PRE-mo
	Prima *(f)*	PRE-ma
Daughter	Hija	E-ha
Son	Hijo	E-ho

English	Español	Guide
Daughter-in-law	Nuera	new-**AIR**-rah
Son-in-law	Yerno	**YAIR**-no
Father	Padre	**PA**-dray
Mother	Madre	**MA**-dray
Father-in-law	Suegro	soo-**A**-grow
Mother-in-law	Suegra	soo-**A**-gra
Niece	Sobrina	so-**BREE**-na
Nephew	Sobrino	so-**BREE**-no
Step father	Padrastro	pa-**DRAS**-tro
Step mother	Madrastra	ma-**DRAS**-tra
Step son	Hijastro	e-**HAS**-tro
Step daughter	Hijastra	e-**HAS**-tra
Granddaughter	Nieta	knee-**A**-ta
Grandson	Nieto	knee-**A**-toe
Grandfather	Abuelo	ah-boo-**A**-low
Grandmother	Abuela	ah-boo-**A**-la
Husband	Esposo	es-**POE**-so
Wife	Esposa	es-**POE**-sa

Para Practicar

Using the verb tener (to have), tell your practice partner how many relatives you have in your family. Start like this: Tengo or I have. Follow that with the number and the member of the family that you are talking about. Tener is covered in the chapter on the five most important irregular verbs in Spanish called the "Big Five" Even though tener isn't a regular verb, it's very practical. You will use it mucho.

Domestic Violence — Violencia Doméstica

Culturally, one of the most important things in Latin American life is *la familia.* Families spend as much time as possible together, and they are very close-knit. It's not uncommon to see the whole family shopping, going to church or walking together in *el parque.* Family members depend heavily on each other and support each other —no matter where they are. The family is so important that personal decisions are often based on the needs of the entire family, rather than the needs of one individual.

Children are the corner stone of the Latin American family. They play a very important role in it from an early age. *Los niños* often become the family's translators. Because children pick up languages so quickly, you will often see them translating for their parents — even in very delicate "adult" situations. Hispanic parents are extremely proud of their bilingual children, particularly if they are limited in English proficiency. These children are the future leaders of their generation.

For many Hispanics in the US domestic abuse is on the rise, in spite of centering cultural values on families and children. Sadly, according to a recent study at the University of South Carolina, 70 percent of Hispanic women surveyed said they were victims of domestic violence. Nationwide surveys also show that Hispanic women are more likely to be victims of domestic abuse than others. A common tactic for abusers to use is to isolate their victims. For Latin American women who speak only Spanish and work inside the home, this is easy to do. Their isolation is intensified by the fact that their families can be in other countries far away from them. For these women, there is no network of help and support, which puts them at an even greater risk.

Hispanic culture places great value in maintaining the family's integrity and its reputation. While this is a wonderful cultural value, sometimes a female, Hispanic victim of domestic violence will not seek help because she fears it will bring shame upon her family. The guilt many women feel often prevents them from seeking help. To further complicate the issue, studies also indicate that many Hispanic victims are unaware that resources exist which will help them escape and rebuild their lives.

In volatile situations like these, use the following questions to get more information about *¿Qué pasó?* (What happened?). Most of these important questions are designed to give you a *sí* or *no* answer in return.

English	Español	Guide
How many people are here?	¿Cuántas personas están aquí?	coo-WAN-tas pear-SEWN-nas es-TAHN ah-KEY
Are there any children here?	¿Hay niños aquí?	eye NEEN-yos ah-KEY
Are there any weapons?	¿Hay armas?	eye ARM-as
Where are they?	¿Dónde están?	DON-day es-TAHN
Show me.	Muéstreme.	moo-ES-tray-may
Are there any drugs in the house?	¿Hay drogas en la casa?	eye DRO-gas in la CA-sa
Was he/she drinking?	¿Estuvo tomando alcohol?	es-TOO-vo to-MAHN-doe al-co-HALL
Does he/she take drugs?	¿Toma drogas?	TOE-ma DRO-gas
Does he/she have a history of mental illness?	¿Tiene una historia de enfermedad mental?	t-N-a OO-na ees-STORE-ree-ah day in-fer-me-DAD men-TAL
Are you hurt?	¿Está herido?	es-TA air-REE-doe
Do you need a doctor?	¿Necesita un doctor?	nay-say-SEE-ta oon doc-TOR
Where does it hurt?	¿Dónde le duele?	DON-day lay do-A-lay

English	Español	Guide
Did he hit your children?	¿Les pegó a sus niños?	lace pay-**GO** ah seus **KNEE**-nyos
Do you want to press charges?	¿Quiere acusarle a su esposo?	key-**AIR**-ray ah-coo-**SAR** ah sue es-**POE**-so
You need to see the magistrate.	Necesita visitar al magistrado.	nay-say-**SEE**-ta v-see-**TAR** al ma-**HEES**-trah-doe

Tips & Tidbits

1. According to the National Institute of Health, intimate partner violence (IPV) is a major public health problem in the US. 17% of Hispanic couples surveyed reported an incident of male-to-female partner violence in the 12 months preceding the survey.

2. Among Hispanic couples the rate of female-to-male partner violence is also high. In the NIH survey, 15% female-to-male partner violence was reported among white couples, 30% was reported among black couples, and 21% in Hispanic couples.

3. Risk factors for IPV are strongly related to socioeconomic factors, alcohol abuse. Domestic violence is both a national and worldwide crisis. According to a 2000 UNICEF study, 20-50% of the female population of the world will become the victims of domestic violence.

4. Abused women and girls often experience adverse mental health conditions such as depression, anxiety, and low self-esteem.

5. The Department of Justice reports that Hispanics are victims of overall violence at a higher rate than non-Hispanics.

Child Protective Services

American society is becoming increasingly sensitized to the tragic phenomenon of child abuse. Politicians, social service and criminal justice professionals along with other responsible parties are under increasing pressure to develop and implement policies that will both protect the public and provide critical assistance to America's youngest victims. Sadly child abuse and neglect can happen anywhere and every child is vulnerable — no matter what ethnicity or race they are. Even though research on racial and ethnic factors on violence and sexual abuse against children is limited, the National Institute of Health is beginning to undertake regular surveys and reporting. Recent studies found that if child sexual abuse occurs in a Hispanic family, the family is more likely to report a family member as the perpetrator and will experience significant guilt themselves as a result. The guilt stems from feelings of not  adequately protecting the child, not from reporting the abuse In the NIH study Hispanics were also more likely to take action in response to the abuse, especially those who were more acculturated.

If you have to investigate a possible case of child abuse or neglect within your Hispanic community, introduce yourself to the child with these phrases.

Hi!	¡Hola!
I'm (your name).	Soy _____.
I'm a social worker.	Soy un/una trabajador(a) social.
I'm sorry.	Lo siento.
I speak a little Spanish.	Hablo poco español.
Do you speak English?	¿Hablas inglés?
Speak slowly, please.	Hable más despacio, por favor.
Thanks.	Gracias.

After introducing yourself, go slowly and with sensitivity to build rapport. Establishing trust is critical to getting the information you need to protect this potential victim. Chances are very good that this child is scared to speak with you. Patience, kindness and good observation will let you know where and when to begin your questions. Start with some of the questions and phrases listed below. If the child is in school, there is a good probability that he/she will have some skill in English, which will be an asset in this difficult situation.

English	Español	Guide
How old are you?	¿Cuántos años tienes?	coo-AN-toes AN-yos t-N-aces
What grade are you in?	¿En qué grado estás?	n kay GRA-doe es-TAS
What is your teacher's name?	¿Cómo se llama tu maestra?	CO-mo say YA-ma too my-A-stra
Where do you live?	¿Dónde vives?	DON-day V-vace
Do you have bruises?	¿Tienes moretones?	t-N-ace more-ray-TONE-ace
Do you have burns?	¿Tienes quemaduras?	t-N-ace kay-ma-DO-rahs
Do you have cuts?	¿Tienes cortaduras?	t-N-ace core-ta-DO-rahs
Do you have scars?	¿Tienes cicatriz?	t-N-ace see-ca-TREES
Please tell me how the accident happened.	Favor de cuéntame cómo el accidente pasó.	fa-VOR day coo-AINT-ta-may CO-mo el ax-see-DENT-tay pa-SO
Do you want to tell me?	¿Quieres contarme?	key-AIR-race con-TAR-may
Do you get hit every day?	¿Te pegan todos los días?	tay PAY-gan TOE-does los D-ahs
Do they kick you?	¿Te dan patadas?	tay dahn pa-TA-dahs

59

Speaking with Parents

Disciplining children physically and ideas on the best ways to raise children differ greatly from culture to culture. In many Spanish-speaking countries, parents are still accustomed to disciplining their children the "old-fashioned" way through corporal punishment. Spanking is a very common practice. It's not unusual for Hispanic parents to feel they have a right to administer this type of punishment and in some cases they may feel it is expected of them.

In many Latin American countries corporal punishment is not prohibited by law and is tolerated or overlooked by the authorities. To further complicate this issue, many Latino clients are unaware of the laws governing physical child abuse in the United States. In many areas Spanish-language newspapers, radio and television stations are conducting public service campaigns to inform their audience about the strict legal statutes governing the protection and rights of children in the US.

Generally speaking, if corporal punishment is administered in a Latin American home, the *madre* usually takes care of it first. However, if the misbehavior becomes more serious or frequent, the *padre* may be asked to step in. Latin American moms are like many around the world. Who hasn't heard at least once, "just wait until your *father* gets home"?

If physical abuse is suspected and a home visit is required, bear in mind that you will most likely speak with the man of the house first. In some cultures, speaking with a man's wife or children requires his permission and you will be unable to fulfill your obligations if you fail to begin your discussion with him.

For the child's safety, if placement outside the home is required, the following phrases will help you explain what is happening to the parents. Keep them handy and practice them often.

English	Español	Guide
I'm here because there is a report of child abuse.	Estoy aquí porque hay un informe de abuso de niño.	es-**TOY** ah-**KEY** pour-kay eye oon een-**FOR**-may day ah-**BOO**-so day **NEEN**-yo
I'd like to see your child.	Quisiera ver su niño.	key-see-**AIR**-rah ver sue **KNEE**-nyo
Do you leave your child alone a lot?	¿Deja su niño solo mucho?	**DAY**-ha sue **NEEN**-yo **SO**-low **MOO**-cho
I need to look at the child to see if there are any bruises.	Necesito mirar el cuerpo de su niño a ver si hay moretones.	nay-say-**SEE**-toe me-**RAR** l coo-**AIR**-po day sue **NEEN**-yo ah ver see eye mo-ray-**TONE**-ace
It's possible we will have to go to a hospital.	Es posible que tengamos que ir a un hospital.	es po-**SEE**-blay kay ten-**GA**-mos kay ear ah oon os-p-**TAL**
If there are no bruises or marks, you don't have to worry.	Si no hay moretones o golpes, no tiene que preocuparse.	see no eye mo-ray-**TONE**-ace oh **GOAL**-pays no t-**N**-a kay pray-oh-coo-**PAR**-say
We get false reports, but we have to investigate.	Recibimos informes falsos, pero tenemos que investigar.	ray-see-**B**-mos een-**FOR**-mace **FALL**-sos **PAY**-row ten-**NAY**-mos kay een-ves-t-**GAR**
How did the child get hit?	¿Cómo lo pegó?	**CO**-mo lay pay-**GO**
Why does your child have so many bruises?	¿Por qué tiene su niño tantos moretones?	pour kay t-**N**-a sue **NEEN**-yo **THAN**-toes mo-ray-**TONE**-ace
Was he/she hit with	¿Lo pegó con	low pay-**GO** con
belt	Cinturón	seen-to-**ROHN**

English	Español	Guide
Extension cord	Cuerda eléctrica	coo-**AIR**-da a-**LEC**-tree-ca
Stick	Palo	**PA**-low
Are there burns	¿Hay quemaduras?	eye kay-ma-**DOO**-rahs
How often has your child been hurt this way?	¿Cuántas veces estaba herido su niño en esta manera?	coo-**WAN**-tas **VASE**-aces es-**TA**-ba air-**REE**-do sue **KNEE**-nyo in es-**TA** ma-**NAY**-rah
You have lost all control.	Ha perdido todo control.	Ah pear-D-doe TOE-doe con-**TROL**
You must speak with a counselor.	Tiene que hablar con un consejero.	t-N-a kay ah-**BLAR** con oon con-say-**HAIR**-row

Tips & Tidbits

Some Latin American families are traditional and conservative. The family structure may be patriarchal with the husband or father holding the authority and ultimate responsibility for the well-being of the entire family. In this type of arrangement the wife's primary role is caring for the children and the home. The concept of *machismo* in which men are seen as strong, authoritative figures definitely plays a role in this view of gender roles and family. While *machismo* and traditional views may still be active in some Spanish-speaking countries, in everyday life among Hispanic Americans they are not frequently a reality. In most *casas* women are important contributors to decision making and wield a great deal of authority in subtle and direct or indirect ways.

Placement Outside the Home

If your home visit finds evidence of *abuso* or *maltrato* of children and they need to be removed from the home for their safety, these phrases will help you explain the process and get vital *información*.

English	Español	Guide
If possible we try to place your child in the home of a relative.	Cuando es posible, tratamos de poner su niño en casa de parientes.	coo-**WAN**-doe es po-**SEE**-blay tra-**TA**-mos day po-**NAIR** sue **NEEN**-yo in **CA**-sa day par-e-**N**-tays
Foster home	Casa hogar	**CA**-sa oh-**GAR**
The judge decides what should be done.	El juez decide lo que se debe hacer.	l who-**ACE** day-**SEE**-day low kay say **DAY**-bay ah-**SER**
When we determine that there has been abuse, we don't have any alternative.	En una situación de abuso, no tenemos alternativa.	in **OO**-na see-to-ah-see-**ON** day ah-**BOO**-so no ten-**NAY**-mos al-ter-na-**T**-va
The child needs protection.	El niño (la niña) necesita protección.	l **NEEN**-yo nay-say-**SEE**-ta pro-tec-see-**ON**
We are authorized to give them that protection.	Estamos bajo la obligación de la ley de proveérselo.	es-**TA**-mos **BA**-jo la oh-blee-ga-see-**ON** day la lay day pro-**VEER**-say-lo
Do you have any close relative here?	¿Tiene parientes aquí?	t-**N**-a par-e-**N**-tays ah-**KEY**

English	Español	Guide
I need their names, telephone numbers, and addresses.	Necesito sus nombres, números de teléfono y direcciones.	nay-say-SEE-toe seus NOM-brays, NEW-may-rows day tay-LAY-fo-no e d-wreck-see-ON-ace

Please Call a Doctor!

If you should find yourself in a situation where you are evaluating the possibility of abuse in children or the elderly, quick reactions and good communication will be essential to handling the crisis. Listed below are laymen's terms for the parts of the body. Learning these parts of the body will help you in emergency situations — and could help you save a life!

English	Español	Guide
Ankle	Tobillo	toe-B-yo
Arm	Brazo	BRA-so
Back	Espalda	es-PALL-doe
Body	Cuerpo	coo-AIR-poe
Brain	Cerebro	say-RAY-bro
Chest	Pecho	PAY-cho
Chin	Barbilla	bar-B-ya
Ear	Oreja	oh-RAY-ha
Eye	Ojo	OH-ho
Face	Cara	CA-ra
Finger	Dedo	DAY-do
Foot	Pie	P-ay
Hand	Mano	MA-no
Head	Cabeza	ca-BAY-sa

English	Español	Guide
Heart	Corazón	core-ra-**SEWN**
Knee	Rodilla	row-**D**-ya
Leg	Pierna	p-**YAIR**-na
Mouth	Boca	**BOW**-ca
Nail	Uña	**OON**-ya
Neck	Cuello	coo-**A**-yo
Nose	Nariz	na-**REECE**
Skin	Piel	p-**L**
Shoulder	Hombro	**OM**-bro
Spine	Espina	es-**P**-na
Stomach	Estómago	es-**TOE**-ma-go
Throat	Garganta	gar-**GAN**-ta
Toe	Dedo del pie	**DAY**-doe del **P**-a
Tooth	Diente	d-**N**-tay
Wrist	Muñeca	moon-**NAY**-ca

Tips & Tidbits

The Spanish word *"seguro"* is used in many important phrases. Even though this word actually means "insurance," it is also a part of the translation of "Social Security." In Spanish that's *"seguro social"* (say-**GOO**-row so-see-**AL**). This phrase is one of the many in our two languages that don't translate identically. It is more of a "concept" translation than a literal one. Most Latin American countries don't have "social security" or other public assistance programs, so our Social Security is viewed as being a sort of "social insurance." Review the following phrases where the word *"seguro"* is used.

1. Medical insurance   Seguro medico
2. Dental insurance   Seguro dental
3. Disability insurance   Seguro de incapacidad
4. Social security   Seguro social

The Body — El Cuerpo

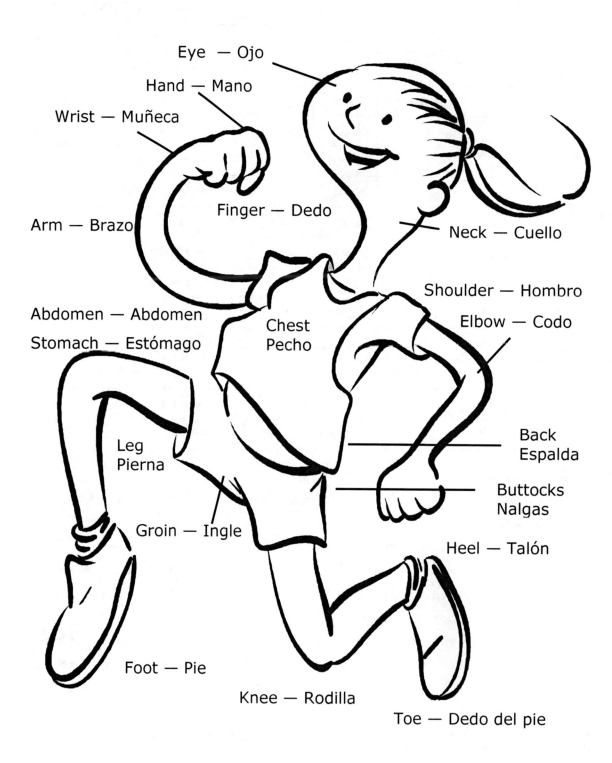

Eye — Ojo

Hand — Mano

Wrist — Muñeca

Finger — Dedo

Arm — Brazo

Neck — Cuello

Shoulder — Hombro

Abdomen — Abdomen

Elbow — Codo

Stomach — Estómago

Chest
Pecho

Back
Espalda

Leg
Pierna

Buttocks
Nalgas

Groin — Ingle

Heel — Talón

Foot — Pie

Knee — Rodilla

Toe — Dedo del pie

The Face — La Cara

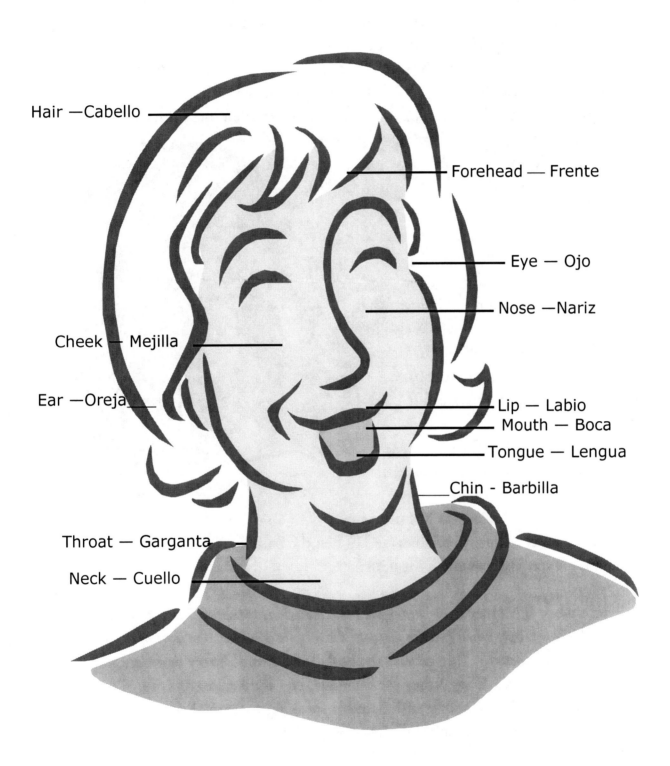

Hair —Cabello

Forehead — Frente

Eye — Ojo

Nose —Nariz

Cheek — Mejilla

Ear —Oreja

Lip — Labio

Mouth — Boca

Tongue — Lengua

Chin - Barbilla

Throat — Garganta

Neck — Cuello

Are You in Pain? — ¿Tiene Dolor?

A few years ago I was honored by being invited to attend the birth of a friend's child. "Carmen," who grew up in Puerto Rico, is completely bilingual, but Spanish is her first language. She has amazing fluidity in her speech and never stumbles in either language. Watching the miracle of birth was amazing — but hearing the affect the physical discomfort had on Carmen's ability to speak English was even *more* eye-opening. The more pain Carmen endured, the more difficulty she had speaking and translating English. As the baby's head appeared, the three nurses who were present all said something different in English. "Push!" "She's almost here!" "It won't be long now!"

At the same time the doctor was attempting to explain to Carmen what was happening. Her sister was also in the room; she was speaking to Carmen in Spanish. Her husband was there too trying to comfort her in English. It was a cacophony of noise! Finally, when she had had enough Carmen shouted, "Shut up! I need to hear the doctor. The rest of you just please shut up. Spanish is still my first language." When the pain increased, thinking in both languages was just too much for her.

That's when it hit me. *Even under the best conditions speaking a foreign language can be a challenge, but, when intense physical discomfort is added, the level of difficulty increases exponentially.* Pain pushes the body to its limits. Every nerve ending is working over-time. Even if they are bilingual, you must take this into consideration when working with Spanish-speaking patients. Because of the physical discomfort they are suffering, you must give them more time to translate from English to Spanish. They are also going to have more difficulty remembering English words, *even if they've been speaking English their whole lives.*

68

When a Spanish-speaking patient discusses pain and discomfort, it's expressed differently than it is in English. Rather than *being* in pain, *en español* you *have* pain. Refer to the chapter on irregular verbs for more uses of tener. Frequently, you will hear the words *tengo dolor*, which means *I have* pain. This phrase is followed by the word for the affected area. When you are asking if the patient is in pain, use the phrase *¿tiene dolor?*

English	Español	Guide
Does it hurt?	¿Le duele?	lay do-**A**-lay
Where?	¿Dónde?	**DON**-day
Show me.	Indícalo.	een-**D**-ca-low
It hurts.	Me duele.	may do-**A**-lay
They hurt.	Me duelen	may do-**A**-lynn
Do you have pain?	¿Tiene dolor?	t-**N**-a doe-**LORE**
Do you have a lot of pain?	¿Tiene mucho dolor?	t-**N**-a **MOO**-cho doe-**LORE**
Is the pain mild?	¿Tiene dolor moderado?	t-**N**-a doe-**LORE** mo-dare-**RAH**-doe
Is the pain intermittent?	¿Tiene dolor intermitente?	t-**N**-a doe-**LORE** n-ter-me-**TEN**-tay
Is the pain deep?	¿Tiene dolor profundo?	t-**N**-a doe-**LORE** pro-**FOON**-doe
Is the pain constant?	¿Tiene dolor constante?	t-**N**-a doe-**LORE** con-**STAN**-tay
Is the pain burning?	¿Tiene dolor quemante?	t-**N**-a doe-**LORE** kay-**MAN**-tay
Is the pain severe?	¿Tiene dolor muy fuerte?	t-**N**-a doe-**LORE** foo-**AIR**-tay
Is the pain throbbing?	¿Tiene dolor pulsante?	t-**N**-a doe-**LORE** pull-**SAN**-tay

Motivation and Evaluation

Many federal programs require appraisals at regular intervals, and they are very important for both the case worker and the client. Everyone appreciates knowing where they stand and getting some positive feedback! When evaluating a Latin American client, keep these important tips in mind:

1. Make sure to get up from your desk. Then, walk around it to greet your client and shake hands. Indicate where you wish them to sit.

2. If your office has a seating area away from your desk, take advantage of it. By sitting in a chair beside your client, you will put him at ease. This removes the desk as an obstacle between you.

3. Don't "cut to the chase" and begin your evaluation immediately. Have some conversation first. Ask about your client's family. A little informal conversation will put both of you more at ease and help you build a better relationship

4. After you have completed your evaluation, ask for your client's opinion. Your Hispanic client will welcome the opportunity to share ideas with you openly.

After you study this section of vocabulary, review your agency's evaluation form. What words from this chapter could help you? Start a form in Spanish to help you prepare for these important conferences. You'll feel better knowing you are prepared!

> Don't let your desk become a barrier for good communications. Get up and sit beside your client. If that's not possible because of the furniture arrangement in your office, move your chair beside your desk or in front of it.

English	Español	Guide
It's…!	¡Es…!	es
Excellent	Excelente	x-see-**LEN**-tay
Fantastic	Fantástico	fan-**TAS**-t-co
Good	Bueno	boo-**WAY**-no
What good work!	¡Qué buen trabajo!	kay boo-**WAYNE** tra-**BAA**-ho
Very good!	¡Muy bien!	mooy BN
You're very important!	¡Usted es muy importante!	oo-**STED** es mooy m-por-**TAN**-tay
You learn quickly.	Aprende rápido.	ah-**PREN**-day **RAH**-p-doe
I respect you.	Le respeto.	lay race-**PAY**-toe
You are very valuable.	¡Usted es valioso!	oo-**STED** es val-ee-**OH**-so
There is/are…	Hay...	eye
Opportunity	Oportunidad	oh-por-too-knee-**DAD**
Great potential	Gran potencial	gran po-ten-see-**AL**
Obvious progress	Progreso obvio	pro-**GRES**-oh **OB**-v-oh
Positive feedback	Reacción positiva	ray-ax-see-**ON** po-see-**T**-va
Realistic goals	Metas posibles	**MAY**-tas po-**SEE**-blays

Tips and Tidbits

Two core cultural values to Latin Americans are "*respeto*" and "*personalismo*." Both are extremely important in any business settings. A professional in almost any endeavor is highly respected. He or she is treated with the utmost courtesy because of the high degree of education they have achieved or their position within in an organization. Age is also an important factor in "*respeto*."

On the Telephone

Talking on the telephone with Spanish-speaking clients is one of the most challenging skills to develop. There's no body language or facial expression from your client to help you. The best way to start this process is to stay as organized as possible. Think carefully about the kind of calls you make to your English speaking clients. What are the phrases you say most often and the typical responses from your clients? Learn these phrases first. Remember it is better to use some of the phrases from page 14 to help you if you get in a jam. There's nothing wrong with saying, *"Repeta, por favor. Habla más despacio."* Make a script to help you get started with telephone skills. This will help you build your confidence.

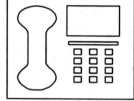

English	Español	Guide
800 number	Número de ochocientos	NEW-may-row day OH-cho-see-N-toes
Answering machine	Contestador telefónico	con-tes-TA-door tay-lay-FOE-knee-co
Area code	Código de área	CO-d-go day AH-ray-ah
Ask for this number.	Pida este número.	p-da ES-tay NEW-may-row
Cellular phone	Teléfono celular El cel	tay-lay-FOE-no say-YOU-lar el cell
Collect call	Llamada a cobro revertido	ya-MA-da ah CO-bro ray-ver-T-doe
Conference call	Llamada de conferencia	ya-MA-da de con-fer-WRENN-see-ah
Could you call later?	¿Puede llamar más tarde?	poo-A-day ya-MAR mas TAR-day

English	Español	Guide
Dial this number.	Marque este número.	MAR-que ES-tay NEW-may-row
Extension	Extensión	x-ten-see-ON
Fax	Facsímile	fax-SEE-meal
Hang up the telephone.	Cuelgue el teléfono.	coo-L-gay el tay-LAY-foe-no
He / She isn't here.	No está aquí.	no es-TA ah-KEY
He/she will call back later.	Llamará más tarde.	ya-MAR-rah MAS tar-DAY
Headset	Auriculares con micrófono	ow-ree-coo-LAR-es con me-CROW-foe-no
Hold a moment,	Espere un momento, por favor.	es-PEAR-ray oon mo-MEN-toe pour fa-VOR
I have the wrong number.	Tengo el número equivocado.	TANG-go el NEW-may-row a-key-vo-CA-doe
I'd like to leave a message.	Me gustaría dejar u nmensaje.	may goo-star-REE-ah day-HAR oon men-SA-je
I'll transfer you to	Le voy a transferir a	lay voy a trans-fair-REAR ah
I'm calling about	Estoy llamando acerca de	es-TOY ya-MAHN-doe ah-SER-ca day
Is this the correct number?	¿Es el número correcto?	es el NEW-may-row co-WRECK-toe
It's very important.	Es muy importante.	es mooy m-pour-TAHN-tay
Local call	Llamada local	ya-MA-da low-CAL
Long distance	Larga distancia	LAR-ga dees-TAN-see-ah

English	Español	Guide
May I speak to	¿Puedo hablar con	poo-**A**-doe ah-**BLAR** con
Press this number.	Oprima este número.	oh-**PRE**-ma **ES**-tay **NEW**-may-row
Repeat that please.	Repítelo, por favor	ray-**P**-tay-low pour fa-**VOR**
Switchboard	Conmutador	con-moo-ta-**DOOR**
Telephone number	Número de teléfono	**NEW**-may-row day tay-**LAY**-foe-no
The connection is bad.	La conexión está mala.	la co-nex-see-**ON** es-**TA MA**-la
The line is busy.	La línea está ocupada.	la **LEE**-nay-ah es-**TA** oh-coo-**PA**-da
The number is disconnected.	El número está desconectado.	el **NEW**-may-row es-**TA** des-co-neck-**TA**-do
There is a phone call for _____	Hay una llamada para _____.	eye **OO**-na ya-**MA**-da **PA**-ra _____.
Two way radio	Radioteléfono portátil	ra-d-oh-tay-**LAY**-foe-no pour-**TA**-teel
Wait for the tone.	Espere por el tono.	es-**PEAR**-ray pour el **TOE**-no
Would you like to leave a message?	¿Le gustaría dejar un mensaje?	lay goo-star-**REE**-ah day-**HAR** oon men-**SA**-he
You have the wrong number.	Tiene el número equivocado.	t-**N**-a l **NEW**-may-row a-key-vo-**CA**-doe
Your name, please	Su nombre, por favor	sue **NOM**-brey pour fa-**VOR**
Your number, please	Su número, por favor	sue **NEW**-may-row pour fa-**VOR**

Clothing — La Ropa

Many social services departments and non-profit agencies also work with clothing distribution. After a natural disaster or other emergency, helping a family find the clothes it needs can be a big help in getting them back on their feet. Everyone will be worried about making sure *los niños* get what they need first. Use the list below to help everyone in the family find something useful.

English	Español	Guide
Bathing suit	Traje de baño	**TRAH**-hey day **BAH**-nyo
Belt	Cinturón	seen-too-**RHONE**
Blouse	Blusa	**BLUE**-sa
Boots	Botas	**BOW**-tas
Dress	Vestido	ves-**T**-doe
Gloves	Guantes	goo-**AHN**-tays
Handkerchief	Pañuelo	pah-new-**A**-low
Hat	Sombrero	som-**BRAY**-row
Jacket	Chaqueta	cha-**KAY**-ta
Jeans	Jeans	jeans
	Vaqueros	va-**KAY**-rows
Overcoat	Abrigo	ah-**BREE**-go
Pants	Pantalones	pan-ta-**LONE**-ace
Pajamas	Pijamas	p-**HA**-mas
Raincoat	Impermeable	eem-pear-may-**AH**-blay
Robe	Bata	**BA**-ta

English	Español	Guide
Sandals	Sandalias	san-**DAL**-e-ahs
Scarf	Bufanda	boo-**FAHN**-da
Shirt	Camisa	ca-**ME**-sa
Shoes	Zapatos	sa-**PA**-toes
Shorts	Pantalones cortos	pan-ta-**LONE**-ace **CORE**-toes
Skirt	Falda	**FALL**-da
Sneakers	Tenis	**TAY**-knees
Socks	Calcetines	cal-say-**TEEN**-ace
Suit	Traje	**TRAH**-hey
Sweater	Suéter	sue-**A**-ter
Tie	Corbata	core-**BA**-ta
T-shirt	Camiseta	ca-me-**SET**-ta
Umbrella	Paraguas	**PA**-ra-**AH**-goo-wahs
Underwear	Ropa interior	**ROW**-pa een-tay-ree-**OR**
Vest	Chaleco	cha-**LAY**-co

Tips & Tidbits

1. Dollars and cents are *dólares y centavos* (**DOE**-lar-es e cen-**TA**-vos). Think back to what you learned about the Spanish sound system. Why does the Spanish word for dollar only have one "*l*"? You're right! The "*ll*" is one of four additional letters in the Spanish alphabet and it always sounds like an English "*y*."

2. For Hispanic consumers, price isn't always the driving factor in where they choose to shop. According to a Nielsen study in 2002, Hispanic consumer's reasons for deciding where to shop were: freshness, cleanliness, friendly employees, low prices, and high quality. Hispanic clients equate the ability to speak Spanish with friendliness.

Giving Directions

The ability to give directions in *español* is one of the most practical skills you can develop. As you direct clients from one agency or department to another, these words will really be a *grande* plus to your conversational ability. You will definitely use these words over and over again. Slowly, you can start to learn this important vocabulary by knowing simple things, such as the four directions: north, south, east, and west. Then, add turns like right and left. Before you know it, you'll be able to give directions to places around town and in your office. This practical vocabulary is easy to practice because you can work on it anywhere you go!

English	Español	Guide
Where is…?	¿Dónde está…?	DON-day es-TA
North	Norte	NOR-tay
South	Sur	SUE-er
East	Este	ES-tay
West	Oeste	oh-ES-tay
Above	Encima	n-SEE-ma
Aisle	Pasillo	pa-SEE-yo
Avenue	Avenida	ah-vay-KNEE-da
Behind	Detrás	day-TRAHS
Down	Abajo	ah-BAA-ho
Here	Aquí	ah-KEY
In front of	En frente de	n FREN-tay day
Inside	Adentro	ah-DEN-tro
Near	Cerca	CER-ca
Next to	Al lado de	al LA-doe day

English	Español	Guide
Outside	Afuera	ah-foo-**AIR**-ah
Over there	Allá	ah-**YA**
Straight ahead	Adelante	ah-day-**LAN**-tay
Street	Calle	ca-**YEA**
There	Allí	ah-**YE**
To the left	A la izquierda	ah la ees-key-**AIR**-dah
Turn	Doble	**DOE**-blay
To the right	A la derecha	ah la day-**RAY**-cha
Up	Arriba	ah-**REE**-ba

Tips & Tidbits:

Neither the names of businesses nor the names of streets are translated into Spanish.
The proper name of your agency is its brand or trade-mark and should not be translated. Consequently, the name of a street is its proper or given name and should not be translated either.

In most Latin American cities, numbers and the words street and avenue are commonly used in addresses as they are in most metropolitan areas of the US. It's not uncommon to find 5th Avenue or 52nd Street. But, our neighborhood streets…well, that's another story entirely! Street names like Taniger Lane, Red Fox Run, or Wood Stork Cove are impossible to translate from one language to another. You should be aware; however, that sometimes a Spanish-speaking person will give you the number of their street address *en español*. Simple numbers are one of the most important sets of vocabulary you can have!

Calming Clients — Calmando Clientes

Building a good relationship with Latino clients is what good customer service is all about. The path to starting that relationship often begins with a smile and a simple phrase or two. When you speak Spanish to your Latino clients, you send a message to them that they are important and that you appreciate them. Using your Spanish may also build your client's self-esteem. On the following list you will find some great "one-liners" that will help you get started. Talking to parents about their children is a great way to start. Practice these often and have fun! You should get lots of smiles and encouragement from everyone!

English	Español	Guide
Don't worry.	No se preocupe.	no say pray-oh-**COO**-pay
Good luck!	¡Buena suerte!	boo-**WAY**-na **SWEAR**-tay
Calm down	¡Cálmese!	**CAL**-may-say
How pretty!	¡Qué bonito! *(m)* ¡Qué bonita! *(f)*	kay bow-**KNEE**-toe kay bow-**KNEE**-ta
He's precious! She's precious!	¡Es precioso! *(m)* ¡Es preciosa! *(f)*	es pray-see-**OH**-so es pray-see-**OH**-sa
What a smile!	¡Qué sonrisa!	kay son-**REE**-sa
Have a nice day!	Tenga un buen día.	**TEN**-ga oon boo-**WAYNE** D-ah
How old is your baby?	¿Cuántos años tiene su bebé?	coo-**AN**-toes **AN**-yos t-**N**-a sue bay-**BAY**
What's your baby's name?	¿Cómo se llama su bebé?	**CO**-mo say **YA**-ma sue bay-**BAY**

One for the Road: Phrases to Use Any Time

Obviously, conversation is made up of more than just lists of words. It will take practice and determination for you to achieve free-flowing conversation in a language that's new to you. Learning Spanish is a slow and steady process for adults. It could take several months before you begin to "think" in Spanish, so don't expect to achieve native speaker speed overnight. There will be times when you feel like you can't remember anything you've studied. That's natural. It happens to everyone. Try not to be discouraged. The rewards you'll receive from learning to speak Spanish are far greater than a little bit of frustration. If you keep working, it won't be long before you'll have a breakthrough. Learning Spanish is a lot like eating a great steak. You don't want to rush it. Cut each bite of your Spanish, chew it over carefully, and savor each morsel. Moving along at a slower pace will help you retain what you learn longer.

Spanish is a language that has loads of zest and flair. It is punctuated with single words and short phrases that can really express a lot of sentiment. The next time you have an opportunity to observe native speakers, listen carefully. You may hear them switch from English to Spanish, depending on what they are saying. And, you might hear them use any of the "one-liners" listed below. Phrases like these add spice to your conversation. Use the following list to help you take your conversational skills to the next level.

English	Español	Guide
Are you sure	¿Está seguro? (a)	es-**TA** say-**GOO**-row
Excellent	¡Excelente!	x-say-**LENT**-tay
Fantastic	¡Fantástico!	fan-**TA**-stee-co
Good idea	Buena idea.	boo-**A**-na e-**DAY**-ah
Happy birthday	¡Feliz cumpleaños!	fay-**LEASE** coom-play-**AHN**-yos

English	Español	Guide
Have a nice day	Tenga un buen día.	TEN-ga un boo-WAYNE D-ah
I agree	De acuerdo.	day ah-coo-AIR-doe
I believe so	Creo que sí.	CRAY-oh kay SEE
I'm so glad	Me alegro.	may ah-LAY-gro
I'll be right back	¡Ahora vengo!	ah-OR-ah VEIN-go
I'm leaving now	¡Ya me voy!	ya may VOY
That's OK	Está bien.	es-TA b-N
It's important	Es importante.	es eem-pour-TAHN-tay
It's serious	Es grave.	es GRA vay
It's possible	Es posible	es po-SEE-blay
Like this	¿Así?	ah-SEE
Maybe.	Quizás.	key-SAHS
Me, neither	Yo tampoco.	yo tam-PO-co
Me, too	Yo también.	yo tam-b-N
More or less	Más o menos.	mas oh MAY-nos
Really	¿De veras?	day VER-ahs
Sure	¡Claro!	CLA-row
That depends.	Depende.	day-PEN-day
We'll see you.	Nos vemos.	nos VAY-mos

Tips & Tidbits

Use short phrases to spice up your conversation. Start with one phrase per week and see how many different situations you can occur where you can use your "phrase of the week."

Typing in Spanish on Your Computer
Inserting Letters with Shortcut Keys

When you need to type letters with accent marks or use Spanish punctuation, you will use keys that you have probably never used before! Actually, you are *composing characters* using the **control** key. It is located on the bottom row of keys. You will see that it is such an important key that there is one on both sides. It keeps the computer from moving forward one space so that the accent goes on *top* of the letter instead of *beside* it.

Always remember to hold the control key down first. It will be the *key* to your success in word processing Spanish. With a little practice these keys will become a normal part of your word processing skills.

Also, if using MS Word, you may use the menu command Insert>Symbol.

To insert	For a PC, Press	For a Mac, Press
á, é, í, ó, ú, ý Á, É, Í, Ó, Ú, Ý	CTRL+' (APOSTROPHE), *the letter*	OPTION + e, *the letter*
â, ê, î, ô, û Â, Ê, Î, Ô, Û	CTRL+SHIFT+^ (CARET), *the letter*	OPTION + i, *the letter*
ã, ñ, õ Ã, Ñ, Õ	CTRL+SHIFT+~ (TILDE), *the letter*	OPTION + n, *the letter*
ä, ë, ï, ö, ü, ÿ Ä, Ë, Ï, Ö, Ü, Ÿ	CTRL+SHIFT+: (COLON), *the letter*	OPTION + u, *the letter*
¿	ALT+CTRL+SHIFT+?	OPTION+SHIFT+ ?
¡	ALT+CTRL+SHIFT+!	OPTION + !

82

Basic Information
Please Print

Date: _____
Month   Day   Year

Mr.
Mrs.
Miss_____
     First Name   *Middle Name*   *Paternal Surname*   *Maternal Surname (Husband)*

Address:_____
     Street

_____
City   *State*   *Zip Code*

Telephone: **Home** _____   **Work**_____

     Cell_____   **Fax** _____

Email Address: _____

Social Security Number: _____-_____-_____

Name of other children: _____

Date of birth   _____
     Month   Day   Year

Driver's License Number: _____

Occupation: _____

Place of employment: _____

Marital Status: ☐ Married   ☐ Single
     ☐ Divorced   ☐ Separated
     ☐ Widow

Husband's name: _____
     First Name   *Middle Name*   *Paternal Surname*   *Maternal Surname (Husband)*
Wife's name: _____

     First Name   *Middle Name*   *Paternal Surname* *Maternal Surname (Husband)*

In case of emergency: _____   Telephone: _____

Signature: _____   Date: _____

Practicing What You Have Learned

Practice is an important part of the language learning process. The more you include practice in your daily routine, the more comfortable and fluent you will become.

The key to practicing Spanish is to set realistic goals. Don't let the language learning process become overwhelming to you. Yes, there is a lot to learn, and it will take some time. But, by setting realistic goals, you have a greater chance of sticking with it. Each of us has different learning styles, so find out what works best for you and break the material down into small pieces. Some of us learn best by listening. Others need to write the words and phrases in order to visualize them. Generally the more of your senses that you involve in the learning process, the faster you will retain the information. Focus and practice one thing at a time. It's doing the little things that will make the greatest difference in the long run. Working five minutes every day on your Spanish is *mucho* better than trying to put in an hour of practice time only once each week. Consistency in your practice habits is vital to your success.

Here are some practice tips that have worked for me and others who have participated in *SpeakEasy's Survival Spanish*™ training programs over the last few years.

1. Start practicing first thing in the morning. The shower is a great place to start. Say the numbers or run through the months of the year while you wash your hair. If you practice when you start your day you are more likely to continue to practice as the day progresses.

2. Use your commute time to practice. Listening to CDs, music and Spanish language radio stations will help you get the rhythm of Spanish. It will also increase your vocabulary.

3. If you are stopped in traffic, look around you for numbers on billboards or the license tags of the cars in front of you to help you practice. Don't just sit there—do something!

4. Investigate sites on the internet. Sites such as www.about.spanish.com and www.studyspanish.com are great places to practice and to learn, not to mention the fact that they are free!

5. Buy Spanish magazines or pick up Spanish newspapers that are published in your area. Many magazines like *People* have Spanish versions and almost every community in the country has a Spanish language newspaper or two. Many of them are free.

6. If there aren't any Spanish newspapers in your area, you can find a variety of publications from Latin America on the internet. Major cities in Latin America all have newspapers that are easy to find on-line.

7. Practice as often as possible, even five minutes a day will help.

8. Don't give up! You didn't learn English overnight and you won't learn Spanish that way either. Set realistic goals and don't go too far too fast.

9. Learn five to ten words each week.

10. Practice at work with a friend.

11. Read! These books will make great additions to your library.

Baez, Francia and Chong, Nilda. *Latino Culture.* Intercultural Press, 2005

Einsohn, Marc and Steil, Gail. *The Idiot's Guide to Learning Spanish on Your Own.* Alpha Books, 1996

Hawson, Steven R. *Learn Spanish the Lazy Way.* Alpha Books, 1999.

Reid, Elizabeth. Spanish *Lingo for the Savvy Gringo.* In One Ear Publications, 1997

Wald, Susana. *Spanish for Dummies.* Wiley Publishing, 2000.

About the Author

Myelita Melton, MA

Myelita Melton, founder of SpeakEasy Communications, remembers the first time she heard a "foreign" language." She knew from that moment what she wanted to do with her life. "Since I was always the kid in class that talked too much," Myelita says, "I figured it would be a good idea to learn more than one language — that way I could talk to a lot more people!" After high school, she studied in Saltillo, Mexico at the *Instituto de Filológica Hispánica* and completed both her BA and MA in French and Curriculum Design at Appalachian State University. She has studied and speaks five languages: French, Spanish, Italian, German, and English.

"Lita's" unique career includes classroom instruction and challenging corporate experience. She has won several national awards, including a prestigious *Rockefeller* scholarship. In 1994 she was named to *Who's Who Among Outstanding Americans*. Myelita's corporate experience includes owning a television production firm, working with NBC's Spanish news division, *Canal de Noticias,* and Charlotte's PBS affiliate WTVI. She continues to broadcast with WDAV, a National Public Radio affiliate near Lake Norman in North Carolina where she lives.

In 1997 Myelita started SpeakEasy Communications to offer industry-specific Spanish instruction in North Carolina. The company is now the nation's leader in Spanish training, offering over thirty of *SpeakEasy's Survival Spanish*™ programs and publications to companies, associations, and colleges throughout the US.

Lita is also a member of the National Speaker's Association and the National Council for Continuing Education and Training. Many of her clients say she is the most high-energy, results-oriented speaker they have ever seen. As she travels the country speaking on cultural diversity issues in the workplace and languages, she has truly realized her dream of being able to talk to the world.

CPSIA information can be obtained at www.ICGtesting.com
Printed in the USA
BVOW04s0822150515

400535BV00013B/4/P